Beneath the

Memoir of a R

by J L Feakin (nee Gabbott)

Memoir – a memoir (/ˈmɛmwɑːr/; from French: mémoire: memoria, meaning memory or reminiscence) **a nonfiction narrative writing based in the author's personal memories**

It is said that we all have a book within us … and this is mine.

I dedicate this book to my boys who have helped challenge and shape me into who I am today. I ask you as my children to open wide your hearts. With love always and forever.

With thanks also to Mum who made sure I got my facts right, something she's always sought to do, and for both her, Vikki Turner, Uncle Andrew Jagels and Iain Wight for their invaluable proofreading. Thank you also to the family members who supplied me with additional details of the events and stories covered and for their encouragement.

All poetry contained within these pages was written by my late father-in-law, Andrew Feakin, who passed away on the 16th March 2019, aged 75. Over his lifetime he wrote over 6,000 poems, many of them truly inspiring, he said the poems 'simply streamed out of him'. Before he passed away I assured him that I would continue to further the reach of this amazing gift.

Contents

Preface

It is known that our formative years shape us for life. For some it is difficult to look back, but for those who do, it can be a very cathartic experience. We all have a story to tell and the art of story-telling needs a revival.

The motto that became popular after the Manchester bombing event in May 1997 was 'don't look back anger' made famous by Manchester Band, Oasis. The song tells the story of a woman called Sally who looks back over her life without regret as she metaphorically reviews the pages of her life. The tune became an anthem of defiance in the face of the bombing.

Whatever our story, to look back with impartiality, enables us to see that we would not be who we are without the events and circumstances that have occurred. Our lives are like a tapestry. We often can only see the reverse side with the hanging threads and its jumble of patterns and colours, but what is forming can be the most beautiful picture - if we let it and if we open our heart and eyes to see.

This is my story, my memoir. A recollection of my memories with their interesting connections linking the past with the present. It covers what life was like as a Catholic girl of Italian Irish descent with my former years growing up in Rochdale. At the age of 9, I became an army kid.

With this new status I began a series of moves to other regions of the UK and to other countries, resulting in being sent to boarding school at age 12. I have often been asked throughout my life, 'what was life like at boarding school?' Some chapters of this book answer that question.

After leaving school I pursued my heart by travelling and working in many different posts in the Americas and then back in England, eventually landing where I started. I have discovered along the way that life often forms a full circle.

When I began to research the history of my town of birth – Rochdale - I found it had its own fascinating story to tell. I have included some local and historical information of the town and the other places that I have been associated with.

Following the trail of my pathway I have recalled some humorous anecdotes along the way. 'Laughter is the sun that drives winter from the human face,' said Victor Hugo. I have found that to laugh is to help dissolve our problems and there are few things more bonding that to laugh with another.

Each of us has a spark of life inside of us, and our highest endeavour ought to be to set off that spark in another – Ralph Waldo Emerson.

My hope is that this book sets off a spark within you...

Chapter One ∞ And so it Begins

The amber glow of the lights below filtered through the thin cotton curtains of the eleventh floor of Holland Rise. As I lay there, the gonging chime of the Rochdale Town Hall clock rang out. I started to count. One.. two .. three .. four .. five .. six .. seven .. eight .. nine .. ten … eleven. Nana came into the room to get into the bed next to mine. As she got into her nylon nightie, static electricity sparks lit up the darkness, firing off all around her. I always thought Nana was electric.

Mum started her nurse training in 1974 and as she would work the long shifts I would spend a lot of my childhood staying at Nana's flat. She had moved to what locally is known as the 'Seven Sisters', following her separation from Grandad. The Seven Sisters consist of seven high-rise tower blocks. In 1963, out of the ashes of an area that was formerly home to a Victorian slum, there appeared 772 flats; four 21 storey blocks containing 476 dwellings and three 17 storey blocks containing 286 dwellings. The flats have a poor reputation now, but when they were first built they were quite futuristic with under-floor heating and modern art murals at the entrance to every block. They were unveiled as a symbol of the town's determination to emerge from its dark industrial past into a bright new world.

Nana Maria and Grandad Ronnie were simply incompatible. Nana had a fiery Italian temper, which had thankfully tempered by the time she became a nana to me, and Grandad was a true Irishman who liked a tipple. Their marriage had been a turbulent one.

I arrived into the world at Birch Hill Hospital in Wardle, Rochdale on the 30th June 1971. My parents decided to name me Joanne Louise Marie Gabbott. Dad's mother wanted me to be called Marie, no doubt after Mary the Mother of Jesus, but they compromised by adding it as a middle name. In the 1970s Joanne was the sixth most popular name in England. The name Gabbott was carried to England following the Norman Conquest of 1066. It comes from a Germanic name from 'gari', meaning spear, and 'bodo', meaning messenger.

My mother and father met when they were teenagers. It was 1970 and they were both working in Rochdale's first and newly opened Asda store, which had been built on a former mill yard in Castleton. It was here that the first automatic tills were tested before being installed nationally in all Asda stores across the country. Dad was four years older than Mum and was on summer break from his teacher training course at St. Mary's College in Twickenham, London, which he soon had to abandon. The college had a deep heritage in education going back to 1850 and is the country's oldest Roman Catholic University.

Rochdale sits ten miles north east of Manchester, nestled at the base of the Pennine Hills. From the view out of my window where I am sitting, I can see the Pennine Way on the West Yorkshire and Greater Manchester border. Termed the 'backbone of England', the Pennine Way is a national trail stretching 268 miles from Edale in Derbyshire to Kirk Yetholm just inside the Scottish border. The Pennine Way briefly links with the Rochdale Way, a 42-mile circular route around the Borough. In the valley below me is the Rochdale Canal, a stretch of the canal network that was opened in 1804 to establish a link for the industrial areas between Manchester and Leeds. This was replaced by the railway in 1839 and the canal system became unkempt until it was restored in 2002.

On the 1st of April 1974, Rochdale left Lancashire and became part of Greater Manchester, with a merger of Heywood and Middleton along with the urban districts of Littleborough, Milnrow, and Wardle. When I was researching for this book I found that Rochdale has quite a fascinating history with some prominent characters being born here.

The Story of Rochdale

In the eighteenth century, it was the centre of the northern cotton trade, and by the nineteenth century, it was known as the mill town 'where plenty of wealthy mill owners and cotton merchants live'. Its location means that it receives more than its annual share of rainfall. The damp conditions prevented the cotton fibres from splitting, which was why it was decided to build so many mills in this region.

Still today it seems to have its own micro-climate. It can be sunny two miles down the road and still raining in

Rochdale. Yet from this location, being at the centre of industrialisation, Rochdale was able to teach the rest of the world how to adapt to progress in manufacturing and mechanisation.

It is also known for being the birthplace of many initiatives including the Co-operative movement, which was founded by 28 residents in response to inflated prices and adulteration of foodstuffs. These 'Rochdale Pioneers' opened their celebrated Co-operative shop on Toad Lane in the centre of Rochdale four days before Christmas in 1844. It started with a skimpy offering of a few pounds of butter, six sacks of flour, one sack of oatmeal, and 24 candles.

However, these Pioneers changed commerce forever with their seven guiding principles standing for political neutrality and equality. The idea of co-operation is for the business to be owned by its customers with everyone working together for a common good, rather than the pursuit of profit. When it was founded it was a time when a pound of tea cost a full day's wage, and wealthy merchants would mix flour with ground bone and tea with ground iron to sell to the poor. This new shop allowed people to buy quality goods at a lower price whilst receiving a dividend for their loyalty. These principles changed the world forever bringing social responsibility to business.

Rochdale was a major influence in heralding reforms internationally as well as locally. The town was known as a clearing house for ideas on the world map. One such reform was in adult education. The Pioneers were not just interested in the welfare of the working classes but also in their learning. In 1850 advanced classes were offered to adults primarily associated with the cotton industry but by the 1880s it had expanded to incorporate many subjects from botany to mechanical drawing and physiology with French. In 1882 the very first City and Guilds exams were held at Toad Lane and in 1884 there were over 100 libraries, newsrooms, and lectures enrolling 2,253 students locally. These initiatives built the foundations of the higher education system in England.

In later years Rochdale Training and Enterprise Council (Rochdale TEC) administered publicly funded training programmes such as the Youth Training Scheme (TYS) and Modern Apprenticeships (MAs) and in 1995 Rochdale TEC became my employer.

On my way to primary school every morning I would walk from my house on Mizzy Road across Cronkeyshaw common and down Whitehall Street. This common had historically been the scene for many political meetings. During the industrial revolution advancements in technology caused skilled workers to fall out of work and into poverty, their jobs now being done by machines.

The country was governed by the wealthy landowner aristocracy and everyone wanted equality and electoral reform. The middle-class wanted parliamentary reform to have the same power that the Tory upper-class had by birth-right. They decided that the only way to achieve this was to create a grassroots movement with the support of the working class.

The working class joined in the struggle in an attempt to improve their living and working conditions. Throughout this period, life in Rochdale was characterised by riots and strikes over food shortages, pay, and working conditions. Parliamentary reform was finally established in 1848 when the People's Charter was introduced allowing the right of almost all adults to vote in political elections, providing one had a sound mind and was not a criminal.

In this season of discontent it became apparent that the only way forward for working-class people lay in self-improvement, it was this decision that led to Co-operation and the birth of the Co-operative movement. By 2012 it had grown and had over a billion members in 100 different countries worldwide. People come to Rochdale from all over the world to visit the original shop in the Pioneers Museum and to learn about the foundation of this Co-operative movement.

Along with the Industrial Revolution and the campaign to support the right of all adults to be able to vote, there was another major force contributing to the changing the face of Rochdale, England and in other parts of the world; namely the church.

People had started to experience a great awakening that brought a deep sense of personal accountability and redemption by Christ alone, rather than dependence on the established church. It drew people away from ritual and ceremony making religion more of a personal experience. The new style of sermons and the way people practiced their faith, such as reading their Bibles at home and social action, breathed new life into religion across England and America.

The church was also the early driving force for the establishment of hospitals and schools, with all schools beginning as Sunday schools. These Sunday Schools were first set up in the 18th century to provide education to working children.

As well as mill-work there was also a mining industry in Rochdale for over 150 years up to the early 18th century. Sadly these were synonymous with child exploitation with children from as young as five years old being sent down the shafts. Though there were no official records kept the death rate was phenomenal. Sunday Schools enabled hundreds of thousands of children to be taught reading, writing, and arithmetic, a system that was a forerunner to our national education system.

There is a back street in Rochdale called John Ashworth Street which runs parallel to Halifax Road. I pass by it quite often and I decided to find out why this man had a street named after him. I discovered that his only education had been received at one of these Sunday Schools. He was born on 8th July 1813 in Cutgate, Rochdale, and was the eighth child of his parents, who were poor woollen weavers. In his early twenties, he experienced somewhat of a spiritual awakening and although he had trained as a painter and decorator, he felt compelled to become a local preacher. He became increasingly concerned for the conditions of the poor and in December 1848 he founded a Ragged School (schools that welcomed society's most destitute children).

After the death of his wife, he went to London where he visited palaces, and prisons and said, 'It was the house for the destitute that interested me more than all...'.

Ashworth felt a calling and believed it was his duty to help the poor, who were being sorely neglected. He vowed on his return to Rochdale that he would go in among them, meet them on their terms and provide them with a place of learning and worship suitable for them. He had two thousand leaflets printed which stated:

> 'Ye houseless, homeless, and friendless;
> Penniless outcasts, COME;
> In rags and tatters, COME;
> Ye poor, maimed and blind, COME;
> of whatever colour, or nation;
> Creed or no creed, COME;
> All we seek is your welfare, both body & soul.'

Ashworth carried on an almost unique work, preaching for the next eighteen years to large congregations, visiting the sick and fallen, spending his money on some of the poorest and saddest cases, and helping many broken men back on their feet. This work introduced him to several 'characters' and John put pen to paper and began to write about the people he had encountered. Sixty-one stories were published and over 3 million copies were sold some being translated into 5 or 6 languages. His most notable book 'Strange Tales' provides interesting glimpses into the life of the poor of Rochdale during this time.

Rochdale today is often in the news for all the wrong reasons, yet there are a few celebrities who have placed it firmly on the map. One is Lisa Stansfield who was born in Rochdale in 1966. Her single 'All Around the World' became a worldwide chart-topper in 1989. She has sold over 20 million albums and also went on to develop an acting career. Another famous actress is Anna Friel who was also born in Rochdale in 1976. Her acting career started when she was 13 years old, and she has since starred in numerous films and British and American TV series. Anna has one daughter whom she named Gracie after another famous Rochdalian, Gracie Fields.

Early Years

Birch Hill Hospital, where I was born, had been a former workhouse in the 1800s. It had also been used by the military in the First World War, joining the NHS as a hospital in 1948. I was the product of a teenage pregnancy. Mum said the whole experience was so traumatic she resolved to never go through with it ever again, and she never did. Due to her age, the midwives treated her terribly. Dad's mother was a strict Catholic and had ushered them both into a shotgun wedding at Sacred Heart church in Rochdale on 5th December 1970.

That evening, after a brief reception at the Kingsway Hotel, they took the ferry to Northern Ireland to spend their honeymoon at my Great-grandma's house in Carrickfergus. Mum's Mum and Dad, Nana and Grandad had also previously gone to Great-grandma's for their honeymoon. I broke with tradition and went to Tenerife.

It was clear that Dad's teacher training plans would have to fall by the wayside. After I was born, Mum and Dad had a petrol station, Plumpton garage on Bolton Road in Bury. They sold fuel and had a shop in which they sold car accessories such as air fresheners, windscreen wipers, and car shampoo. Mum also worked at the Launderette on Oldham Road in Rochdale a few days a week, taking me along with her in my pram. On certain afternoons Mum would work at the petrol station and Dad would take me home leaving her to carry on working the pumps. Those were the days when a garage attendant would fill your car with fuel. In the shop they also sold car batteries, which is how Dad met Eric, who owned Elton Batteries down the road. A few years later Dad bought Eric's battery shop.

The Italian Connection

Mum was one of three siblings from immigrant parents. The eldest of them was Elvira, who had been named after Nana's mother, and the youngest named Michael after Nana's father. Nana had travelled from a small village called Baranello, in the Molise region of Italy, whilst Grandad had come from Belfast in Northern Ireland. Nana was the eldest of six children. When she was just 24, her mother, Elvira Terranova, passed away with cancer and it was then that Nana decided to seek work in Britain, which she did in 1950.

Nana was born in 1923. The previous year, Benito Mussolini had been appointed the Italian Prime Minister by King Victor Emmanuel III. Mussolini wanted to restore the former glory of the Roman Empire and embarked on a series of events leading to Italy becoming a one-party dictatorship. It gained control of other countries including Ethiopia and the pre-existing territories of Italian Somaliland and Eritrea, although they launched attacks on many others. Mussolini's resistance in joining the allied forces in the Second World War inevitably caused his dismissal and he was put in custody. He was later rescued by German paratroopers and Hitler placed him in charge of a puppet regime in Northern Italy. In Nana's native region was the Winter Line – a series of German and Italian fortifications representing Germany's last line of defence in the country.

With the demise of Mussolini, Italy was able to flip sides to the allied forces. This put many of their troops around the world and their own people at home in a difficult position. Nana's memories of this time were of exchanging her hens' eggs for cigarettes with the German soldiers and of her mother, who was the village seamstress, sewing the soldier's shirts. The Germans went from being friends to enemies overnight.

The Irish Connection

Grandad was born in Belfast in 1929 at the start of the troubles. He was the eldest of three siblings, his sister Pat and brother George; both emigrated to America and lived in Brooklyn, New York for many years. Grandad Ronnie had been born very prematurely and they did not think he would survive. Great-grandma had previously had a late miscarriage and was determined that he would live. Auntie-Vi, Great-grandma's sister bathed him in olive oil and wrapped him in cotton wool and he was placed in a shoebox in the hearth range and fed droplets of milk, much like you do when you find a tiny bird. However, survive he did and he went on to live to the grand old age of 81.

When I was a child, we took quite a few visits to Northern Ireland catching the ferry from Liverpool. Great-grandma lived in a small cottage on Robinson's Row. Out of my bedroom window, I had a clear view of Carrickfergus Castle across the road. I still remember the taste of fried soda bread with cooked tomatoes from the full Irish breakfast she would make us every morning. Once or twice we would go into Belfast shopping. It was the 70's and the troubles were very much apparent. Before going into a department store, we would have to line up and have our bags searched by police officers with an imposing array of guns. It felt a very threatening atmosphere.

Centuries ago, Ireland came under British rule. As a result, Scottish and British nationals settled there, mainly in the north. At the start of the twentieth century, there was a quest to break the link with Britain and become a republic. However, the majority in the north wanted to retain the link with Britain and so in 1920 the land was divided. There followed decades of violence in an attempt to end British rule and become one united state. Over 3,500 have been killed in the troubles with many more traumatised and thousands imprisoned. Since the 1990s however there has been a period called the 'Peace Process' in which much of the violence has stopped.

My Irish Great-grandma Amy was a warm, down-to-earth character. She was always cheerful and non-judgmental; she simply got on with life whilst allowing others to get on with theirs. All the time she lived at Robinsons Row, up to her death in 1991, she had an outside toilet and no inside bathroom. There were two bowls, one for washing up the pots and one for washing the body, and a curtain that would pull around the kitchen sink to provide some privacy. There are numerous family photos of Amy looking the epitome of glamour at some Christmas party or other, but usually, she would be in a dowdy dress and would leave out her dentures. Every Friday though was shopping day. On these days she would transform her appearance and en-route to the shops would stop by Harbour Bar for a little drink, a pub owned by her sister Winnie and husband Joe.

During the Second World War, the national troubles were put to one side. Due to the bombings in Belfast, Grandad was evacuated to his Auntie Greta's house above a sweet shop that she owned in Carnalea, west of Bangor in County Down. Though I am sure it was a tremendously difficult time for children, being sent to live at your Auntie's who owned a sweet shop, must have been a bit of a bonus.

Great-grandma Amy and Great-Grandad James had met in Scotland whilst working in service, Amy as a housemaid and James as a chauffeur, and they married on 6th July 1927. Later James had a bit of a dark shadow over his life. He had been accused; tried and convicted of murdering his stepmother by hanging her from her kitchen door. He was in Barlinnie Jail in Glasgow awaiting execution when he appealed his sentence. On appeal, the conviction was overturned, and he was released. Grandad remembers the flashbulbs from the local press who were waiting for the family to disembark from the ship as they arrived back in Ireland from Scotland. The last capital punishment was finally abolished in 1969 with the last hanging in 1964. One of Britain's most notable hangmen was called John Ellis. He had been born in Rochdale and had been involved in a total of 203 executions.

James Mills ended up dying nine years later after his merchant navy ship, the Punta Gorda, an Anglo-American Oil Company tanker, was hit by a torpedo from an enemy submarine. All the crew was lost at sea. Following James' death, Great-Grandma had a few admirers. One of them, John Brown, wanted to marry her, but her response was, "Sorry but I'm not giving up my war widow's pension for any man".

Great-Grandma's brother, Uncle Kay had owned a pub on the Old Lodge Road in Belfast. It was in an area caught up in the troubles and eventually he decided to leave and move to the quieter area of Carrickfergus where he lived next door to Great-Grandma. Uncle Kay would take me on walks on our visits and every time we passed a lavender bush, he would take a head of one of the flowers and show me how to rub it between my hands to make it smell like a perfume. I still cannot resist doing that when I pass by some today.

And so they came to Rochdale

Both Nana and Grandad had come to England in search of work and a better future than their native lands could offer at that time, Nana on a two-year work contract. The British government was advertising overseas regarding their need for women to come and carry on the work that British women had done as part of the war effort (post-war they had left the mills and gone back to being housewives). Nana responded to the call and came by train through the mountains of Switzerland finally arriving in the UK. She met Grandad at a hostel for immigrant workers in Chorley and from there they ended up in Rochdale.

Nana, like many others, found work in a local mill, coincidentally just after she had acquired her new surname of 'Mills' from her maiden name of 'Terranova'. The name Terranova means 'new lands' and she had certainly left all that was familiar and ventured into a new land. Grandad had started his working life as a lift attendant in Belfast but had gone on to do a three-year apprenticeship as a sheet metal worker and soon found a job in Rochdale. They were married at Rochdale's registrar office in Rochdale Town Hall on 22nd of August 1951, within a year of meeting.

Exactly one hundred years before I was born, in 1871, John Bright had laid the foundation stone of the Rochdale Town Hall. It is said to be 'one of the finest in the country' and is a Grade I listed Gothic-Style building and cost today's equivalent of £15 million. It has a facia of millstone grit quarried largely from Blackstone Edge. The clock tower reaches 190 feet tall and the stained-glass windows are credited as 'the finest modern examples of their kind', some of which were designed by William Morris. Morris was a famous textile designer, poet, artist, novelist and activist, and the founder of the British Arts and Crafts movement in the nineteenth century. I visited his former home and museum on a recent trip to London.

On the hour, and at every fifteen-minute intervals, five bells of the clock tower of Rochdale Town Hall ring out. It has a floor area of 2,500 meters and an impressive medieval-style grand hall that is lined with statues of angels. Adolf Hitler was so impressed with the Town Hall he declared that after he had won the war, he was going to dismantle it and transport it back to Germany. Rochdale seemed to be largely avoided by German bombers and thankfully the Town Hall still stands where the foundation stone was laid. Usually, on Fridays there are guided tours around this impressive building, and currently, it is undergoing a multi-million-pound restoration programme.

One of the most famous people to ever stand on the Town Hall Balcony is Rochdale's own Gracie Fields. She had been born over a fish and chip shop, owned by her grandmother, on Molesworth Street in 1898. Her first stage appearance was in 1905 and she went on to become a famous London West End star. In 1937 she was the highest-paid film star in the world and was well known for tirelessly flying out to entertain the troops during the Second World War. She contributed more to the war fund than any other star and the Nazis viewed her as Winston Churchill's secret weapon.

In later life, Gracie was a regular feature on the TV show 'Stars on Sunday' in which well-known performers sang hymns and read extracts from the Bible. She eventually retired to Capri in Italy, but always remembered her Rochdale roots and made regular trips home to perform. She died in 1979 and in 2016 a full-size statue of her was unveiled on Rochdale's Town Esplanade to commemorate her life.

Chapter Two ∞ Pressed Beef and Mashed Potato

"Hullo, Hullo is that Amy Mills? Hullo it's your boy Ronnie. How arr ye doin?" The conversation would follow the usual pattern each Friday as Grandad would ring his family back home in Ireland. He would be hunched over Nana's armchair leaning forward with the cream, curly telephone wire extended to the table next to the television. Even after my grandparent's separation, Grandad would come to Nana's for tea every Friday and give her a £10 note.

In an attempt to immerse herself into British life and because Grandad did not like Italian food, Nana seemed to sadly lose much of her Italian culture. I would love for her to have taught me her native language and how to make pasta from scratch. The extent of my knowledge of the Italian language seems to consist of how to count to ten and how to say a swear word – no doubt learned from Nana.

Nana's repertoire of British cooking did not extend far and in an attempt to meet Grandad's palate, every single Friday we would have pressed beef, mashed potatoes, and cut tomatoes. We didn't seem to question it. I would often have dinner with them before heading out to meet my friends in Madison Square Gardens, a pub I could see from Nana's flat window. She passed away in 2008 but I still cannot help but look up towards her flat every time I drive past.

One of my earliest memories is of us going to the Rochdale market on a Saturday morning. Nana liked the second-hand stall and would often come back with "all kinds of tat" as Mum would say, a horse statue made into a clock, trophy jugs, and clay vases. Maybe this is where my love of second-hand shops was formed. We always went to the same food stall each week to buy the pressed beef and some eggs. Eileen and Peter Jordan had been running the stall since 1960. Eileen seemed to be good friends with Nana and they always had a chat. Even after Nana's stroke, we would go down town with her, and Eileen would try and communicate with her.

A few years ago Eileen passed away and Peter Jordan continues to work on his market stall which he has been doing for sixty years. He now sells mainly fresh eggs and plants from the family's farm in Rossendale. Jordan's stall is located on the walkthrough from the Town Flats to the Town Centre and has been trading eggs in Rochdale for over 100 years. Peter's grandfather, Patrick, initially set up the stall on Yorkshire Street in 1919. I still sometimes buy my eggs from Peter just to keep this memory alive. Many of his eggs are also double yokers and who does not like the surprise of one of those?

The same year Mum became pregnant; her older sister Ellie had also become pregnant. Michael and I were born almost four months apart. At the time it must have been quite devastating for Nana to have both her teenage daughters pregnant. Even though Mum and Ellie both got married before we were born, it was a time when neighbours would gossip over the back garden fence. Yet once we arrived in the world she devoted herself to us. My abiding memory is of a nana that always gave us unconditional love and always smelled of bleach. I do not think she was a great believer in any other cleaning product; it was a scent that she carried around with her, like an 'Eau de Parfum'.

Nana had a strange habit of sitting on her armchair backwards and leaning over the headrest. There she would spend many hours reading one of her many Mills and Boon books. She seemed to have the complete library, no doubt picking them up from the second-hand bookstall on Rochdale market. She also had a love of house plants and her flat was full of them, but in particular, she liked cactus plants. Mum said it was because it made her laugh when anyone got spiked by one. She had quite a sense of humour.

One day she had asked us to buy her a spray bottle to keep her plants moist and we had brought it with us. Mum and I had entered into a silly little water fight with it and one of us accidentally got Nana. She seized it from us and pointed it in our direction, only she had not quite managed to turn it the right way round and instead squeezed as hard as she could and sprayed herself in the face with it. I cannot remember if she saw the funny side or not, but Mum and I definitely did.

Occasionally I would go and stay with Grandad who then lived on Ennerdale Road (not to be confused with the TV series). It was near Springfield Park on the Bolton Road which had a running miniature railway that he would often take us to. He liked to go on long walks, something I now also love, but then I dreaded every step. He would walk my cousin Michael and I to Heywood, often calling in at a shop called Bobby Dazzlers. It is only a four-mile round trip but then it felt like I was being asked to walk from John-O-Groats to Land's End.

Grandad liked his gadgets and Bobby Dazzlers was full of them – whistling key finders, mini torches, and microwaveable food containers. Grandad was one of the first people I knew who had a microwave oven. He thought it was the best invention ever and seemed to rapidly build up a collection of every conceivable plastic container that was on the market. He was also a frequent visitor to the Newtown Social Club on Nixon Street in Rochdale. If I happened to be staying with him on a weekend, he would sit me in a corner of the family bar with a packet of crisps and a coke and go and have a game of snooker next door, leaving me with the bar-lady. She was a friendly woman and would replenish my coke when I finished it.

Another place Grandad would take me was to the main library in Rochdale, a place he also used to take Mum when she was a child. I loved the musty smell of the old wood panelling and the sound of the creaky floors under my feet. I would gather a small pile of books and find a quiet corner to while away the time. The library was first built in 1884 after a small fire at Rochdale Town Hall destroyed the Clock Tower Library in 1883. In 1903 the art gallery and museum were added to it. The building was converted into an art and heritage centre in 2003 and renamed Touchstones.

Grandad was quite musical and had several violins. Mum thinks he bought his first one from a lady selling it cheap. When he would practice the flat would resound with the squeaky sound of strings rubbing against the bow. I was quite fascinated by an old wood metronome that sat on his living room red-tiled window ledge. Of course, I did not fully understand what it was back then; I would watch it move from side to side whilst it made a clicking sound at regular intervals.

Grandad loved classical music, and he tried to get me interested by sitting me down to listen to 'Peter and the Wolf', a musical composition written by Sergei Prokofiev in 1936. The narrator tells a children's story, while the orchestra illustrates it by using different instruments to play a 'theme' to represent each character in the story. He was a great fan of James Galway, who had also been born in Belfast. Galway had an international career as a solo flautist player and we later took Grandad to watch him live at the Bridgwater Hall in Manchester in 2003.

Photography was also another hobby Grandad enjoyed, turning their early family bathroom into a dark-room to develop his prints. This love of photography was passed onto Mum and me. I love nothing more than to walk out on the moors or round the Hollingworth Lake with camera in hand, though today we all seem to be able to take photos just as well on our phones.

Rochdale has another first on this theme. The very first war photographer was a man called Roger Fenton who was born at the Crimble Hall estate in Rochdale on the

28th March 1819. The Hall was bought by the Decker group in 1960 and turned into a restaurant which was extremely popular for many years. It has since gone into liquidation and is due to become a housing estate. Fenton was instrumental in founding the Photographic Society and in 1854 he was commissioned to document events occurring in the Crimean War. His ancestor, another Roger Fenton, who had been born in 1565 was one of the original translators of the King James Bible.

I first lived with Mum and Dad at a different kind of estate; Ashfield Valley Flats. It was a £5 million estate that had been completed in 1969. The estate comprised of 1,014 flats in 26 blocks. Initially, it had been a popular place to live, but like many estates, it faced decline over the years. Now, most of it has been demolished with only three blocks remaining. In their place is Sandbrook Park which consists of a cinema, gym, and restaurants.

In 1974 we moved into a three-storey weaver's cottage on Mizzy Road, a type of house that was once used by weavers for cloth production. Dwelling quarters were on the lower floors with a weaving room on the top floor. At the top of the house there was a long row of mullion windows which had been designed to provide maximum light for the weavers. It was built in the late 18th Century by Jacob Bright Snr for his cloth outworkers. Interestingly I also attended a nursery school named after Jacob Bright known as 'Bright's Nursery' on Whitworth Road from early 1974 to attending primary school in September 1975.

Jacob had started a cotton mill in 1809 and his sons continued the Bright Empire after his death. He had also been involved in politics and served as Rochdale Town Mayor and also as MP for Manchester. His son John Bright was born in Greenbank, Rochdale in 1811 and was one of the greatest politicians of the 19th Century, known around the world. Bright won every campaign he fought; from the repeal of the Corn Laws (which protected the higher price of corn for the wealthy British landowners) to taxing the aristocracy in Ireland to alleviate the famine. He also successfully campaigned for Parliamentary reform and promoted free-trade and religious freedom.

Bright is the only politician to have two statues in the Palace of Westminster and his bust is sited at the entrance to the White House in Washington. He is also thought to have been the first person to use the term 'flogging a dead horse' which he used when he was speaking in the House of Commons in March 1859. Bright was also ardently anti-slavery, which brought him into close contact with the American President Abraham Lincoln. They became personal friends and when Lincoln was assassinated, he had a letter of support from Bright in his pocket.

Bright first married Elizabeth Priestman of Newcastle in 1839. They had one daughter named Helen, but his wife Elizabeth died on 10th September 1841 and her death took him to the depths of grief. Cobden, Bright's best friend, and fellow campaigner, spoke some words of condolence, but then said, "There are thousands of homes in England at this moment where wives, mothers, and children are dying of hunger. Now, when your grief is past, I would advise you to come with me, and we will never rest till the Corn

Laws are repealed." From that time on they never ceased to fight on behalf of the poor and afflicted.

John Bright inherited the family cotton-spinning business, the Bright Empire, with his two brothers Jacob Jnr and Thomas. From the small beginnings in 1809, Bright's family business grew massively. At its peak, the Empire consisted of seven mills in Rochdale later producing items as diverse as carpets and belting. In the days of cotton spinning, bales would have been transported by a carrier, spun at the mill, and given out to handloom weavers to weave in the lofts of their own houses, such as in the top room of our own house on Mizzy Road.

Bright was closely associated with the North Wales tourist resort of Llandudno. In 1864, he was there on holiday with his second wife and five-year-old son, Leonard. As they passed through the picturesque graveyard of St. Tudno on the Great Orme, Leonard said, "Mamma, when I am dead, I want to be buried here." Later that day he developed scarlet fever and a week later he sadly died. His wish was granted and a grave was found for him near the church door.

Bright returned to Llandudno at least once a year until his own death in 1889 and he was a great benefactor to the town. There is even a high school named John Bright in honour of him. Llandudno is one of my favourite places, and we spent many a time taking my boys there when they were small to visit their paternal great-grandma who lived nearby. I recently visited St. Tudno's church and decided to find this little grave, it simply reads:

'In loving remembrance of Leonard Bright
who died at Llandudno on Nov 8, 1864, aged nearly 6 years
And There Shall Be One Fold And One Shepherd'.

We did not seem to use the top floor of the house on Mizzy Road where once the weavers would have spent their days, but it had some of my toys up there so I would sometimes go up there to play. I distinctly remember playing with a set of scales to play shop, but it felt a little eerie and I did not go up there too often. Although we had an internal bathroom, the house still had an outside toilet block and sheds and when we moved in, there was an old hermit living in them called Harold. The odd occasion I would see Harold shuffling across our back courtyard surrounded by a cluster of cats that he used to feed. As I type this it sounds completely bizarre. Why did no one call Social Services? But for some reason, Harold and my parents seemed completely fine with the situation and I was assured that he was harmless.

It was at Mizzy Road that I got my first pet, a cat called Cherry. The name was chosen as I thought her nose resembled a cherry. No doubt she was acquired to try and catch the large extended family of mice that ran rampant around our house. I could never have a chocolate Christmas calendar as the one year that I did, they ate from the 1st through to the 24th in one night. Cherry either felt overwhelmed or was vegetarian as a few months later she walked out and never came back. I saw her a few weeks later happily settled on someone else's front room window-sill, no doubt eating a diet of mushroom pate.

Maybe we should have let Harold and his cats live on the top floor, which would have solved the problem in no time.

A few years later in 1975, Dad also walked out and never came back. To minimise this impact on me, whilst Dad was leaving, Mum took me to Redruth in Cornwall to stay with Mrs. Wood. Mrs. Wood had taken Mum and her sister, Ellie, under her wing when they were young, taking care of them whilst Nana was out at work, but she had since moved away. By now Dad had taken over the petrol stations at Birch services on both sides of the M62 between junction 18 and 19. He rented the site from Safe Petroleum and sold groceries in the shop whilst making a profit from the fuel.

Around this time Dad went for an area manager position with Total Oil and there he met Polly; they married in 1978. Dad also returned to his Catholic roots and started attending mass again.

Dad had been raised by my Grandma Gabbott, known as Peggy. She had been brought up in the Cottage Homes Orphanage along with her sister Netta, in Shore, Littleborough on the outskirts of Rochdale. Their mother had died of TB and their father was unable to look after them. Children's cottage homes had sprung up in the late nineteenth century for orphaned, destitute, and abandoned children as a means of preventing children from going into the Workhouses. In England, the Poor Law Unions, which went on to become the local authorities, took the idea from a similar project in Europe that had been very successful. Rather than place children in institutions they built smaller groups of buildings and established them in their own gated 'village'. Many in the early developments had schools, workshops, sports facilities, and chapels.

Throughout England and Wales, there were 43 of these 'villages' established each housing between 100 and 700 children at any one time. The children were all placed in smaller units much like quaint cottages with a foster mother and father. As time went on and funding began to reduce the children started to blend in with the local community, attending the local schools and churches. In 1930 up to 15,000 children had been accommodated at any one time and it is thought the total number of children who had passed through cottage homes was in the region of 175,000. When the Poor Law Unions ceased to exist responsibility for the children was passed to the local authorities.

The Rochdale Union opened their purpose-built cottage homes in Wardle in 1900. There were eight cottages housing 150 children. Eighty children were moved in straight from the workhouse. Each cottage accommodated fourteen children and whilst some in other areas they had been clothed in uniform, here they were allowed to wear ordinary clothes in order to blend with the local children.

My Grandma Peggy married Harold Gabbott, one of three siblings whose own father had been the stationmaster of Newhey train station. Harold had been a POW in the Second World War after being captured by the Japanese. He had worked on the railway depicted in the 1957 film 'Bridge over the River Kwai', or more recently in the film 'The Railway Man'. I only remember him as a frail-looking old man sitting quietly in a chair behind the entrance door of the living room. I would pass him as softly as I could to retrieve the Ribena cordial that Grandma kept in the living room cabinet.

They had three boys and lived at the end house on Westward Ho in Milnrow. Their house was directly adjacent to the grounds of St. James Church of England church. Dad's youngest brother, Mark, who was only 11 at the time, would chase me round and round a pathway that led alongside the graveyard and back into their garden. It would have been a convenient place to attend worship except Grandma was a staunch Catholic. All the boys were altar boys at Sacred Heart Catholic Church and she hoped that one of them would become a priest.

Chapter Three ∞ Porridge with the Nuns

Barefoot on the sand, I could feel the tidal shapes the waves had made on the beach. The sky was turning its sweet pallet of orange and red as the sun was making its descent. As I stared at the sky, Grandma Gabbott said, "Go on - that one was for you, go and get it". I saw my new ball beginning to be taken by the breeze and ran after it, catching it just in time before it was taken away on the wings of the wind.

Grandma Gabbott had been a bit worried she wasn't going to see me following my parent's divorce and decided to take me on a little holiday. I was her only grandchild at that time. We went via coach to a convent called St. Augustine's Priory at Old Colwyn in Conwy, North Wales. In 1939, The Sisters of the Sacred Heart of Jesus and Mary (or the Chigwell Sisters for short) took over the Priory from a community of Augustinian nuns.

It was a five-minute walk from the beach and Grandma Gabbott bought me a ball to play with. We went on the beach as the sun was going down and had a game of football, passing it to each other. If she kicked it to me and I missed she would say, "It was meant for you, so run after it". If I kicked the ball to her and she missed she would say, "You kicked it, so you go and get it". She had me running up and down that beach like there was no tomorrow. I felt she was being a little bit mean at the time, but no doubt it was a tactical method of tiring me out before bed. She also would have been heading towards fifty years old which seemed ancient in those days. Nowadays, of course, it is definitely not old whatsoever!

Each day we would wake up early to the ringing of a bell and would have to go down to early morning mass. This was then followed by eating porridge with the Nuns. I wonder now if they had taken a vow of silence as there was not much conversation taking place, just the scraping of spoons along the bottom of their bowls. The day after buying the ball a gust of wind did take it away and it disappeared from sight. Later on, when I was lamenting the lost ball, probably in the hope she would buy me another one, she said, "Why don't we pray about it?". So we did. As we continued on our walk along Colwyn Bay sea-front suddenly it appeared in a gutter. "There you go!" she said, with a smile on her face. I have to admit I was pretty awestruck. Maybe the seeds of faith were sown in me that day.

My Italian nana would have been more interested in another convent down the road, St. Mary's Convent School. It was where Rita Lewin attended having been evacuated there during the Second World War. She was a prolific writer of romantic fiction, feverishly writing her first novel under the bedcovers by torchlight at the age of 14. She ended up writing more than 100 titles for Mills and Boon, selling more than 25 million books in 23 different languages, tapping into women's hearts all over the world dreaming of romantic love. It seems that 'love' sells but Leigh herself was quoted as saying, "Some people like to go to bed with a man, I like to go to bed with a man-uscript". Over the years I have come to agree with her.

Dad and Polly went on to have another five children, later fostering another seven and resulting in the adoption of one of them. With Polly's two from her first marriage and me from Dad's, it meant there were eight of us altogether in the early days. I would often go to stay on alternate weekends. By now Dad had bought and developed a chain of car battery shops called Eltonite Batteries. Through his contacts in the motor industry, Dad had ended up working with an elderly man called Eric who had a battery shop called Elton Batteries in Bury.

Eric taught Dad all he knew about the battery business then decided it was time for him to retire. Dad subsequently bought the first shop from him for £1,000 in 1976. He then expanded the business and in its prime had shops in Bury, Rochdale, Oldham, and Salford. Throughout Dad's lifetime, his career seemed to alternate between petrol stations and the battery business with a period in between importing Japanese MPVs. Much later he started another new business, Alpha Batteries, based at Spotland Mill in Rochdale, which has experienced significant growth over the years, resulting in it becoming a leading online power solutions company.

Those early battery shops had a distinct smell; a mixture of oil and damp – and it was much like being in a car repair garage but with a shop front window. There seemed to be oil marks everywhere, and various posters from battery manufacturers on the walls. There was a stone-flagged floor and a Calor gas heater in the backroom to keep warm. It seemed just as cold in there in summer as in winter. I was always told not to let my clothes or skin touch anything or the acid would burn a hole in them. Terrified at the thought, I felt like I was a contestant on the Krypton Factor having to negotiate a minefield as I attempted to tread through the shop without my clothes or hands touching anything.

As children, we largely got on well together, and I would go with Dad and Polly and their growing brood on their annual holidays. With so many of us to keep entertained Pontins holiday camps in Southport or Brixham were always a firm choice. I once won the 'Miss Personality' competition. I have no idea what won the judges over, I think I was the only one who did not copy what the last girl said as they went down the line shoving a microphone in our faces. I managed to muster up something just ever so slightly original at the last minute. I still have the photo somewhere. I also have the photo of when Tommy Cooper came to do an act and of me standing next to him – it seemed a big deal at the time.

Day trips were always a feature in those days – the late 70s and early 80s. We would be driven to Southport beach and told to 'get out and play'. We would hit the sand-dunes running. Meanwhile, Dad and Polly would get some much-wanted peace from us all and Dad would read his newspaper. We would make a brief appearance for egg mayonnaise sandwiches at lunchtime and then disappear again. Those sand-dunes made us feel like we had arrived on a completely different planet. We would run up and down them like mad ferrets and occasionally get lost in them not knowing which way was seaward. Often we would appear what seemed like miles away from the car, but would eventually find our way back. Now of course, sadly, children do not have quite the same freedoms.

Polly's mother and father also played a big role in our childhood. Gar, as Polly's dad was affectionately called, worked for Tetley's breweries and would go round the social clubs promoting their beer and performing. He did an incredible act whereby he would dance and sing around the room with a pint of Tetley's beer on his head, not spilling a drop. The song, 'Well Hello, Dolly', seemed to be the one that remains most in my memory. He always won the adult talent competition at Pontins – but then he did have a head start. He was the life and soul of any party, and their house on Dane Road in Sale was filled with Tetley's promotional paraphernalia. Sadly in 1990, he passed away before his time from minor surgery complications, so minor most of us did not even know he had gone into hospital. He left a big hole in the family that has been impossible to replace. However, he did leave us with some very fond memories.

Mum often had friends over to the house on Mizzy Road; one such friend was Marjorie, who was also doing her nurse training at Birch Hill Hospital at the same time as Mum. She would often come over and at the same time Damien, Dad's brother, would be there. One year Damien asked Mum if she would ask Marj if she would go to a Christmas do with him. She said, "Yes I'll go, but make sure he knows it's just that and nothing else". They got married 7 months later.

When I was younger Damien and Marj would sometimes take me out. At one point they had a corner shop selling groceries in Summit, Littleborough and the locals called him Granville (from the TV show 'Open all Hours', a show which ran from 1976 to 1985). Like Granville, Uncle Damien had a girlfriend (wife) who was a nurse and ran a corner shop. He was known for his banter and his practical jokes. The shop was one of the last bastions of the community. Summit was once quite thriving, with a post office, a butcher, a Co-op, a fish and chip shop, and five pubs. Now all have gone apart from the Summit Pub, having been replaced by the nearest supermarket, and with it the decline of the community spirit.

It is a shame they moved on, as forty years later I moved just across the road from their old shop. I would have liked to have lived opposite Granville and Nurse Gladys and been able to pop in for a pint of milk, but they are now enjoying retirement and the shop has been converted into a house.

I currently live in a house that was built in 1896 and sits directly on top of the 2,648-foot long Summit Tunnel, one of the oldest railway tunnels in the world. The railway was established in part to replace the canal transportation system. Rochdale has the highest concentration of canal locks in the north with 91 locks over 32 miles. Just next to my house there are fourteen ventilation shafts of the Summit Tunnel which allowed the steam from the old locomotives to escape. It was completed in 1841 to provide a direct connection between Leeds and Manchester on the trans-Pennine line and is still in use today. When all is quiet at home I can hear the sound of the train's horn in the distance as it enters the tunnel.

On the 20th December in 1984, the tunnel experienced its greatest test. A huge blaze was sparked when a freight train carrying 1 million litres of petrol derailed deep inside the tunnel. It had been a cold winter and ice had formed in one of the shafts which had fallen and affected the rail line. Flames shot 150 feet into the sky from ventilation shafts and temperatures inside the tunnel reached 8,000 degrees centigrade, melting the brick wall and welding the tankers to the track. The Rochdale Observer covered the incident with the headline 'FIRE IN THE HOLE'. George Stephenson, the tunnel's builder, had said, "I stake my reputation and my head that the tunnel will never fail so as to injure any human life". His words proved true and despite the seriousness of the blaze no one was killed. The driver and crew managed to escape and run the one mile out of the tunnel to ring for help. The fire raged for four days and even though it was one of the coldest of winters, the event managed to dupe nature as spring flowers began to bloom on the earth above.

It was the biggest blaze many of the Greater Manchester fire-fighters had ever experienced in their working lives. It took four days up to Christmas Eve before the fire brigade officially could say that the fire was out. Although the tunnel was badly charred, it was repairable. At the start of August that next year locals were allowed a once-in-a-lifetime opportunity to walk through the tunnel before normal rail services resumed.

The old remembered years long past,
of quieter days, of things that last.
The corner shops and village stores,
of friendly neighbours' open doors.
Life was simple, easily planned,
always there, a helping hand.
The pace was slower, people cared,
and the ups and downs of life were shared.
Families then were more secure,
Relationships were stronger, pure.
Times were hard but that was life,
for there was often love in place of strife - AF.

Primary Days

In 1975, I attended St. Patrick's Catholic primary school. The school was part of the Catholic parish of St. Patrick, which had been founded in 1860. It had largely been established by an Irish priest called Michael Moriarty, who lived in Rochdale from 1861 until 1897. He was well known for having an attractive personality but died in a street accident in Nice, France. His body was brought back to Rochdale for a solemn requiem and he was later buried in Ireland. Clearly, he liked to get around. I took my First Holy Communion in the parish church on the 13th of May 1978.

My best friend from school was a girl called Sara Twigger. Sara, my cousin Michael and I had all attended Bright's Nursery together. I was told I enjoyed it there. I do remember we had a slide, a swing, and a metal roundabout inside in the hall. I cannot say I have ever seen an indoor park quite like it before or since, but then it is Rochdale. No doubt the nursery nurses got sick of shouting,"Everyone in, it's spitting!" and decided to bring the playground inside. The afternoon naps were marked by rows of little beds on the floor each with a grey blanket. For some reason I do remember having to eat tapioca which had the consistency of frog spawn, which I struggled to swallow.

Sara lived on the street behind me in the posher, newer houses. She was the youngest of three girls and I was a little envious of her Cindy collection; she had the motorhome. We would go to each other's house on a Tuesday evening, alternating each week. When Sara would come to mine it would be fish fingers, chips, and beans as it was her favourite. When I would go to hers, her mother would make spaghetti bolognaise as it was my favourite. It was nice, but she always put sliced carrots in it which I could never quite understand, and did not have the heart to tell her that it really was unnecessary.

Our home on Mizzy Road was close to Falinge Park, a Victorian park with an old hall, a play park, a duck pond, and large grassy areas, which we would often play in. One day we decided it would be fun to run away together. We could not have got very far, as above the houses, we could hear Sara's dad calling her home for tea. Somehow dads then could be heard shouting for their kids several miles away, but then earphones had not yet been invented. We decided to turn around and go back; I think we got hungry.

Sara and I remained best friends for many years and were together in the 23rd Rochdale Brownie Pack based in the old St. Andrews Methodist Church. This has since been demolished to make way for a new shopping centre and a Hilton hotel. Even after we moved to Plymouth in 1980, Sara would come down on the 883 Yelloway coach and spend time with me over the summer holidays.

Yelloway coaches are an iconic brand associated with Rochdale and its beginnings go all the way back to 1902. In May 1913 the first-purpose-built bus or charabanc entered service, a 28-seat Dennis painted yellow with burgundy upholstery. When it arrived in Rochdale at the offices of Holt Bros a member of staff shouted *"The Yellow Car has arrived!"* from here it was named the Yelloway coaches. By 1984 it was operating regular direct routes to Poole, Swansea, Clacton-on-Sea, Paignton, Southampton, and Plymouth. A Yelloway mini-museum has been built inside a former Yelloway coach by enthusiast David Haddock, which is based at the Bury Transport Museum.

Sara's mother, Gaye, was an amazing seamstress and made many of the banners for St. Patrick's Catholic Church. She would also make most of Sara's clothes. Sara would come down to Plymouth on the coach with her little suitcase neatly packed with the most amazing collection of clothing. What we loved most was to go roller skating. In Rochdale, we would go to Rollercity, a place which is still running almost 50 years later. In Plymouth the place to go was Rollarena, but we would also visit the Hoe, the grassy area, and the walkway by the sea. The Radio One

Roadshow was a key event that we would go to every year, the last of which was held in 2020.

In 1978 Mum bought a house, 78 Brookdale, on the Healey Farm Estate, then a new housing estate. We lived next-door-but-one, to her best friend from school, Linda Griffin. Linda was married to Steve (or Griff as he was affectionately called) and they had three children. Growing up, it was like we were one family, not two. We were always in and out of each other's houses and would go on our annual holidays together to Cornwall, and later on my first beach holiday to Majorca when I was 15.

As Mum was a nurse, I was often at Linda's or at a child-minder called Brenda Lake, who lived in a terraced house on Rivington Street round the corner from my school. There was an old lady always sitting in an armchair in the corner of the living-cum-dining room, who was her mother. There seemed to be lots of old ladies in corners on armchairs back then, but now they all end up in residential homes. We often spent time across the road, in the back living room-cum-kitchen of her friend's wool shop which fronted onto Whitworth Road. I would sometimes go there after school, eat crumpets and watch TV shows like – 'Why don't you?' and 'Mr. Benn' while waiting for Mum to finish her shifts at the hospital.

The school was pleasant enough, but they placed an inordinate amount of importance on church attendance. Every Monday morning the headmaster, Mr. Butler, would come around all the classrooms with a list of all those who had not been spotted in church the previous day. If you were on the list you would have to stand up and give a reason why you had not attended mass. I already felt distinctly like the odd one out as I was the only one in my whole year from divorced parents, so to be additionally singled out for non-church attendance struck abject terror in me. Come what may, I would ensure that I had been spotted genuflecting and doing the sign of the cross at the right time every Sunday morning.

Occasionally, Mum would come with me, but there were times when I would walk to church alone down Whitworth Road just to ensure I got my mark. One time when Mum did attend with me we both got a bad fit of the giggles, the type that you cannot suppress no matter what, all about the enormous hat of a lady who was sitting in front of us. We had been sitting just two rows from the front and I just hoped and prayed we had not been noticed. I did not encourage Mum to come to church with me after that; she had the potential of getting me into too much trouble.

I was frequently ill with tonsillitis as a child. It seemed to recur every few months until I was finally admitted to Birch Hill Hospital when I was 7 years old to have my tonsils removed. I remember sitting up in bed looking at the other children on one long ward, all having had their tonsils and adenoids out, all clutching their teddies. After a few days, we were all discharged. Mum was scared of me having a post-op haemorrhage, as the ex-sister of the ENT (ear, nose, and throat) ward had told her horror stories about it happening.

She hoped it would not happen to me, but that first night home I started haemorrhaging badly from my throat and was readmitted. She had heard me get up in the night and go to the bathroom. She went to see if I was OK, and I was leaning over the loo with blood pouring out of my mouth. She rang the hospital and they told her to get an ambulance but Mum could not wait so she wrapped me up in a blanket and drove me there herself. I would not let them take blood for a transfusion and she heard me say, "No I want my Mummy to do it". Mum came back into the room and took the blood. In the end, it settled with antibiotics.

One day I was off school ill again and, whilst I was away, they chose parts for the Christmas nativity. When I returned to school, they announced that I had been chosen to play the part of Mary. It felt a real honour as I was sitting there with a blue sheet over my head, yet I was terrified that I would drop the baby Jesus and spent the whole experience with a knot in my stomach. One teacher that stuck in my mind was Mr. Simkins; he taught upper Primary and had a strong Irish accent having come from Tipperary. We would reconnect later in life.

Chapter Four ∞ Army Days and the Banging of the
War Drum

"We're getting married", Mum told me with delight. I felt
sheer panic and ran upstairs to the bathroom and locked
myself in. It did not feel as though I was about to gain a
father-figure, but that I was about to lose my mother. I
was nine years old and my life was about to change
completely. Mum's old school friend, David Fitton, who
had joined the army at 16, had returned to Rochdale on
leave and came looking for Mum.

Their first romantic liaison took place in a most
memorable location. When they were 13 years old they
were on a school trip to Rochdale's sewage works when he
first took hold of her hand and held it as they had a tour of
the treatment plant. They used to sit next to each other at
Balderstone Secondary school and David would copy
Mum's maths homework – she still takes care of all his
paperwork and accounts to this day.

He had been raised in Castleton and was one of four
siblings, three boys, and a girl. Castleton was the home of
Rochdale castle until the early 13th century when it was
abandoned. It has since been levelled and built upon.
David's mother, Norma Fitton, had owned the village
hairdressers aptly named 'Norma's' and the family lived
upstairs in a three-bedroom flat. Decades later David went
into the shop, now a sandwich shop, and told them he

used to live upstairs. They asked if he wanted to go up and take a look. He did and was amazed to discover it had the exact same wallpaper in all the rooms from when they all lived there sixty years ago.

In 1980 when he was on leave, he came looking for Mum. Finding that she was now divorced, he proceeded to sweep her off her feet. Within a few weeks, they were married by special licence and we packed up, left all we knew behind and moved 300 miles away to Plymouth in Devon where David was based. It was a shock and I did not react with much positivity at first, yet life took on a very exciting edge and I soon warmed to it. All of a sudden I was an AK or army kid and we moved into our first army quarter on Beverston Way in Southway, Plymouth. Overnight it was like I obtained Bear Grylls for a father. David was in the 59 Commando Regiment and had served with the Paratroopers and had a deep-sea diving certificate. He had an unquenchable thirst for adventure, which he endeavoured to instil in me.

One year we arrived at a ski resort at sundown and wanting to make the most of every minute, David rushed me up the last ski lift. Mum had more sense and stayed at the bottom. By the time we got to the top the sun had gone down and it was pitch black, there are no street lights on the back side of mountains. I had to follow him down a path as closely as I could. We did not realise until the next day, that there had been a sheer drop down one side.

I was pushed down death-defying death slides, put on sea sailing and jet-ski courses, and once canoed around Drakes Island in Plymouth Sound in choppy seas, having never sat in a canoe before in my life. All of which I have to say I did with very little resistance. Being an army kid meant I got to attend family days on the army camp where I could try my hand at rifle shooting and army assault courses. As I got older I was allowed to the Mess Dinners. These were formal events where ball gowns were required and I had to remember every minutia of table manners that had been agonisingly drummed into me over the years.

Anyone getting married from camp got full use of the Army facilities. David was a master chef and was often there organising huge catering events. On one occasion a family friend was getting married. I ended up in the kitchen being presented with the biggest bucket of prawns I had ever seen or since seen, it was my job to peel them all. At every big army event, there would always be the most amazing spread; mounds of food, some in jelly, some things piped, things with cherries on top, and always at the centre a full pig's head with an apple in its mouth. It seemed revolting to me at the time and could not understand why anyone would want that as their table centrepiece.

One year David was asked to organise the catering for the Royal Tournament at the Earl's Court exhibition centre in London. This was the world's largest military pageant which was held by the British Army between 1880 and 1999 and acted as a fundraiser for leading forces charities. I went along and helped set out chairs and to generally lend a hand. It was the only time I have seen the Queen in person. David was in the line-up to meet her as she walked the red carpet to her seat. I was standing in the line just behind the front and could not quite believe just how small she is. I remember reflecting on myself having a dazed look with a gormless, half-smile on my face as she passed; she probably sees that quite often.

After we moved to Plymouth, Mum did not want me to get the train on my own to Manchester. The only option apart from doing the long car ride was for Dad to arrange to fly me back. So when I was 10 years old I solo boarded my first ever flight, a 40-seater Brymon Airways De Havilland Dash 7 aircraft. It was the type of aircraft the man I later married was to pilot in his career. There were no direct flights to Manchester from Plymouth so I had to fly via Heathrow airport. All UM's (Unaccompanied Minors) were brought into a separate space in the airport, which was then an area in the middle of the terminal sectioned off by room dividers. We were allowed to leave this section at intervals and wander around Heathrow airport on our own just as long as we came back. It seems inconceivable now.

We loved living in Plymouth and because it was a seaside town we had lots of visitors. We spent many happy hours on Plymouth Hoe, watching the ships sailing by, visiting the Barbican with its age-old buildings and souvenir shell shops. From there the Pilgrim Fathers set sail in 1620 seeking religious freedom from persecution and the jurisdiction of the Church of England which they felt was corrupt. Grandad loved to get the 883 Yelloway coach down from Rochdale and from those same steps, we would take boat trips to Drake's Island, or up to see the warships in the docks.

My cousin Michael was also a regular visitor to Plymouth. He was a much more willing contender for death slides and rifle ranges and even had his own combat-style pants and top when he was 10. Being around David must have made a huge impact on him, as when he turned 16 he signed up and undertook his army training at Harrogate, finally joining the Signals Regiment. He was deployed in the first Gulf War as part of the British Army Spearhead and was on the first military flight the day Iraq invaded Kuwait in 1990. He remained with the Army until 1992 and served in Northern Ireland in a surveillance unit as an electronic communications specialist. He later came out of the forces and found work in telecoms.

We would often spend Christmases all together. Auntie Ellie and Mum had both become midwives so where we spent Christmas would depend on their respective shift patterns. We all loved going to my Auntie Ellie and Uncle Andrew's house: Nana, Grandad, Mum, David, Michael and his family, me with mine and Mum's brother's children. They always had the biggest house, and Auntie Ellie is a fantastic cook and the perfect host.

The most memorable time was when she had moved to a picturesque village called Grayingham in Lincolnshire. That Christmas morning I took a bike ride through the nearby rural village roads and a gentle snowfall descended from the skies. It felt perfect. Auntie Ellie and Uncle Andrew moved to Brisbane, Australia in 2001 when my uncle was recruited as a top pharmacist for Queensland.

There they were able to connect with Nana's brother, Uncle Pasquale, and his wife Auntie Carmela and their grown-up children. They hoped we would all follow them to Australia, but circumstances did not seem to allow it for any of us, though we had wanted to.

Back in Plymouth it always felt safe on Camp. I saw the camaraderie between the men, the sense of mischief and fun in social times, and yet the absolute sense of duty when the time called for it. On the 2nd of April 1982, Argentinian forces invaded the Overseas Territory of the Falklands Islands, which had been a British colony since 1841. On the 6th of April, Mum and David's first wedding anniversary, David was called up for the war. He was no stranger to conflict having served on five tours of Northern Ireland between 1972 and 1981, seeing many of the troubles first-hand. On this occasion, he was to set sail with the initial task force on the SS Galahad for the 8,000 mile trip from Plymouth. He was responsible for setting up the catering division and feeding the troops. Arguably this is one of the most important front-line tasks for as Napoleon Bonaparte once said, "An army marches on its stomach".

Not long after David had disembarked from the ship it was attacked by three Skyhawks from the Argentinian forces, hit by several bombs, and sunk. The explosions and subsequent fires caused the death of 48 crew and soldiers. He narrowly missed death a second time after arriving on the island. He had been sleeping with many other soldiers in an old agricultural refrigerated warehouse that had been used in the sheep farming industry. The day he moved on this too was hit by bombs and many were killed. It was a ten-week war in which 255 British forces personnel were killed and 775 left wounded. In addition, 649 Argentinian forces and 3 Falkland Island residents were also killed. The Argentinians finally surrendered on the 14th of June 1982. David appears on a photograph in a book entitled 'It's No Picnic' standing next to a huge pile of weapons that had been seized from the Argentinian soldiers.

I recently found a letter David had written to me from the Falklands, by paraffin lamp, describing his conditions, 'the last two days have been absolutely awful, and it hasn't stopped raining at all. We have tightened up the door and I am sat with my wellies on as there are three inches of mud at the bottom of the tent... I am guarding a runway near a place called San Carlos, the countryside here is very much like Dartmoor. There is a small settlement nearby with about eight farm houses and the people are very friendly indeed. Today I swapped an English pound note for a Falklands one, enclosed, for your collection... Time is short now Jo and I am running out of paper, so take care and I hope to see you soon, all my love David xxxx'.

At that time the SS Canberra, an ocean liner, was returning from a world cruise. She was built at the Harland and Wolff shipyard in Belfast, Northern Ireland, the same shipyard that had built the Titanic. She cost a total of £17 million and was part of the P&O fleet from 1961 to 1997. During the Falklands War, she was requisitioned to bring the troops home. It travelled from the South Atlantic archipelago and finally arrived back to the UK on the 11th

July with David and the whole 3 Commando Brigade on board.

Mum and I went to meet him and I remember standing on Southampton Docks at the age of 11 watching the ship sailing in. The decks were flanked with service personnel all waving, with some holding up a banner made from a sheet that read, 'We came, We saw, We conquered'. It is a Latin phrase, attributed to Julius Caesar after his victory in the Battle of Zela on the 2nd August 47BC. It was a very emotional day. A huge flotilla of boats accompanied the ship to harbour and thousands of multi-coloured balloons were released into the sky. The docks were packed with loved ones who had all come to welcome the troops home.

When Mum and David got married, I was halfway through my final year at St. Patrick's primary school in Rochdale and had to start a new school called Widewell Primary in Plymouth. I remember struggling to fit in. I had a northern accent for a start and everyone already had their friendship groups. There was one tall, stocky girl who challenged me to a fight after school simply because I was new. I would like to be able to say I accepted the challenge and won; but I knew I was no match, she was built like a brick house and I legged it home as fast as I could. I think I could have won the Olympic 100 meter gold medal that day if I had been timed. I have always been more of a peace-maker. From there I went to Notre Dame Girl's high school. However less than one year later, David was posted to Munster in Germany, so we packed up and moved again.

On arrival in Munster, we had to get our photo identifications done. The troubles from the IRA were still relatively current and all forces personnel and their families had to have ID badges. Before entering camp, vehicles were still being searched for bombs, holding mirrors under the chassis. In Munster, I was sent to a school called Edinburgh High, which was the nearest school that catered for army kids. In the Second World War it had been a German Barracks and over the reception door still hung an Eagle minus its swastika. There were also cells in the basement of the science block where prisoners had been kept. I was mortified when Mum applied for the position of school nurse and got the job. I was 12 at the time and it was seriously not cool to have your mum work at the same school that you attend. It also meant that I could not get away with anything.

I soon found myself in a group of troublesome friends. Surprisingly for a school full of children from forces families it was completely out of control. The teachers were all civilians and there did not seem to be any discipline or real education taking place. One day Mum passed by and saw me with blue eyeliner smeared under my eyes. It was then that she decided she would have to take action before it was too late.

At that time the army helped to pay for service children to attend boarding school. Taking a recommendation from a Captain Mitchell on camp, we took a quick trip back to England to visit St. Mary's Gate School (SMG) in Southbourne, Bournemouth. We were shown around by Miss. Richardson, who seemed very stern even on a welcome tour. She asked me a question to which I responded with an "OK". She replied with "OK? We do not use Americanisms here, child!" It was the only school we looked at and the decision was made. I was to be sent back to England to start life as a boarder at SMG, where I remained from the age of 12 to 17.

A few months before my 13th birthday I travelled by military plane to RAF Hendon where I spent the night as an Unaccompanied Minor (UM) in the air force base family accommodation. There was a lady spending the night there too in transit to someplace with what looked like about 3 children under 4. She felt a bit sorry for me and took me under her wing. After breakfast the next morning I was put on a train to Bournemouth where I was met by Sid, in his yellow minibus, an old man who was the school driver.

Boarding school was a time to pull up my bootstraps and toughen up. With Mum in a different country and with no mobile phones, I had to learn to deal with issues myself. Yet again I started school halfway through the school year. The girls did not make newcomers very welcome and for a time it was tough. It was as though you had to pass a slow initiation process before you were accepted. SMG was a very hostile environment. Even among us girls throughout the time we were there, we seemed to harden our hearts as to show emotion was to become a target. By the second term, I began to make friends and finally started to fit in.

One of these friends was Lou Moogan, who coincidentally had a huge love of cattle. Her grandmother owned a farm in Gloucestershire where Lou had developed a close relationship with these four-legged friends.

The school seemed to have a strange mix of pupils. The vast majority were forces children; some, however, were from very wealthy families who lived in Jersey and had ponies, and some who declared that they were African royalty. There was also the Chinese cohort who kept to themselves. They would often be found giggling together in a huddle eating their stash of what seemed like very strange food. Lou was also an army kid. Her parents lived just 22 miles away, but she and her sister had been put in boarding school. No doubt her parents, like all the parents, believed it would be best for our education.

Each Friday in assembly, class positions were read out for every single pupil. All our school work was graded and points awarded. Your position in the ranking order would be declared for all to know. Lou was almost always in the top position. Looking back it must have been very demoralising for those with unrecognised education needs to always be coming last and for all to know it. But it was in the day when it was thought that to humiliate people would incentivise them to reach up higher. Now we know different.

Another close friend I had was Isabelle. She was in the Jersey group. Her family had a yacht and one summer, while I was living in Plymouth, they sailed over and berthed it at the Mayflower Marina. This meant we got to see each other, and I spent most of that summer down at the Marina. I loved the sound of the clanging of the masts and the feel of the wooden boardwalks beneath my feet.

At one point there was a big yacht that pulled up in the next berth. It had huge sails and a Polish crew on board and we soon got to be friends. One evening Izi and me were lying on their deck looking up at the stars and drinking a bottle of something, as teenagers do, whilst one of them played traditional folk songs on a guitar. It is moments like these that stick with you. I have liked boats and being on the open water ever since. At the time I was doing a sea sailing certificate at the Royal Marine's Stonehouse Barracks, which was round the corner from the Marina.

Chapter Five ∞ Routine and Shenanigans

'Riiiinnnng, Riiiiinnnnng', the bell was sounding out and it was time to get out of bed, into the chillingly cold air, and get into our uniforms. Being adolescents and having a complete lack of privacy we had developed interesting ways of getting dressed and undressed without showing anything to each other, much like a magician who pulls scarves out of his sleeves. Showering facilities were in a draughty lean-to, and the water was always cold.

St. Mary's Gate (SMG) was a large Victorian house on Belle View Road in Southbourne, Bournemouth. We had to follow a strict, daily regime and our every move was controlled by the bell. It would be rung to wake us up and at every other juncture of the day. In the morning, on the ringing of the first bell, we would have to get out of bed and get dressed. Our clothes would be hanging up at the bottom of our beds with our polished brown lace-up shoes beneath, having been inspected the previous evening. Our bedding consisted of two sheets and blankets, four if you were lucky, and one pillow. Each morning the bedding would have to be stripped and neatly folded on top of the mattress, with the sheets folded in a neat square separately.

The bell would go for breakfast and we would have to silently walk down the right-hand side of the stairs to the dining room. Tables were set in various formations of between 8 and 16 pupils. We would stand by our table and wait for Miss. Richardson, the housemistress, to stomp in. She would stand there for what seemed an age waiting until you could hear a pin drop, and then she would say the grace and sit down, after which we were allowed to sit down. She was a formidable woman who invoked terror in almost all of us. She was a spinster who wore heavy make-up and a Margaret Thatcher-style hair-do. She appeared to thrive in her position of authority and seemed to want to make our lives as miserable as possible.

In the evening by 9:30 pm, lights were out in every dormitory, and she would sneak around the floors with an ear to every door to try to catch someone talking. When she did she would barge in, demand that the guilty stand by their beds whilst she berated them, and eventually would issue an order mark. An order mark meant that you had to do extra chores that weekend instead of being allowed out and she issued them like they were going out of fashion. When we were all asleep, or at least all quiet, she would be able to go home, so on reflection, it is no surprise she was as harsh as she was.

If any of us were ill we would have to go to Matron Holt. She was a sweet, older lady with buck teeth. Whatever complaint we went with, she would apply Witch-hazel. She seemed to believe it was a cure for all. I think even if someone came in with half a leg missing, she would quietly get some cotton wool out of the mirrored cupboard and apply Witch-hazel to it. You would have to be practically concussed to be able to stay in bed and I do not remember anyone ever going to a hospital, though probably some should have.

After breakfast, we would go back to our dormitories and make up our beds with precise hospital corners. They were then inspected by the sixth formers, known as seniors, and if not made to exact standards would be completely re-stripped. We would then be called upon to remake it until it met the requirements.

Being an old Victorian house it was always cold. There was often ice on the inside of our single-paned windows and after school in winter we would all make a mad dash for a huddle with the old fashioned radiators before dinner. The radiators only put out the faintest of heat, so back then we all wore onesies, even before the term was invented. We all seemed to have one complete with thick bed socks and often knitted gloves too. When a storm would pass by we would block up the sides of the sash windows with tissues to stop them rattling all night long and to try to keep the draught out.

Lack of privacy was something that you just had to get used to. In some dormitories, the bunk beds were so jammed together it was impossible to find any space. There were no common rooms or lounges, so our beds were the only place we could sit on in any free time that we had. It was the era of the launch of the Walkman cassette player. We would sit on our beds with our headphones on in our onesies and swoon over posters of the likes of Duran Duran and Wham.

In 1985, the song 'Last Christmas' was released and we would dream of being that girl in the music video snuggling up to George Michael by the fire. Of course we were not allowed to put posters up on the walls, but we would cut pictures out and pin them onto sides of cupboards where they would not be seen by the Gestapo.

It was also the era of the Princess Diana flick. I was born with naturally curly dark hair and seemed to spend most of my childhood figuring out ways of making it straight and flick-able. One Christmas I was given some curling tongs, which may seem strange for someone with curly hair, but if used correctly could, in some fashion give your hair an appearance of being less curly (it was before hair straighteners had been invented). One day I had used my curling tongs when the lunch bell rang, I had switched them off and left them wedged in the chest of drawers to cool down and went down to the dining room.

Miss. Richardson was a little later than normal in her entry that day. Then it happened. She marched in with my curling tongs in hand and raised them above the heads of the 200 girls asking who they belonged to. It felt like I was about to be sentenced to the gallows. I feebly raised my hand and was given an angry verbal barrage about how I had almost burned the school down and I was to receive four order marks. The seniors on my table tutted and gave me condescending looks. Four order marks meant four weeks of extra chores and no going out. Thankfully Dad backed me up and appealed to the school saying that I had no idea curling tongues were against the rules (which was true) and gained me a slightly lighter sentence.

We were only allowed off the premises for four hours on Saturday and again on Sunday. When leaving the premises we had to go out in full dress uniform which included a boater hat, blazer, and white gloves in summer and a felt hat and camel coat or grey cape in winter.

We were often the target of the local children's taunts and would sometimes get tomatoes and eggs thrown at us. Once our group was even flashed at, it was an underwhelming experience. Before leaving the grounds we would have to find a group of two or three other girls to leave with and we were not, under any circumstances, to split from our group. On the way out we would have to face a full inspection to ensure we were wearing our uniform correctly. It felt like we were passing through Checkpoint Charlie.

As soon as we were out, we would all walk as fast as we could to the local red phone box (running was forbidden unless you were playing sports). This was our only chance of speaking to our families. Each Saturday and Sunday for four hours all the local phone boxes would be inundated with uniformed girls surrounding them like bees to honey. We would form an orderly queue and would patiently wait our turn with our white-gloved hands clutching our ten pence pieces.

Sometimes we would walk to the shops in Christchurch or Boscombe which took an hour each way or take a closer jaunt to Pokesdown or Tuckton shops. Two places that were strictly forbidden however, were the beach as 'it was not becoming of young ladies' and Bournemouth town centre, unless you were a senior. When I look back it is astonishing to realise that I lived only a quarter of a mile from the beach for 5 years and I never set foot on it. We could even see the sea from certain dormitories.

On Saturday evenings we were allowed to get into civvies (non-uniform clothes). However, there was a strict rule that no trousers must ever be brought onto school premises. I was generally a well-behaved girl. I had a healthy respect for authority and liked my weekend freedom too much to break the rules. However one day I must have been feeling a little rebellious and Lou and I hatched a plan. We put our civvies on under our uniform and put a plastic bag folded up in our shoes. We would leave with a group who we would make swear an oath of silence, find a big bush, and strip off our uniform placing it in the plastic bag from our shoe and get on the next bus to Bournemouth. It seemed fail-proof.

After passing the inspection team, with our hearts in our mouths, we carried out our plan and jumped on a passing bus. We felt invincible and wandered around Bournemouth feeling like we had just escaped from a maximum-security prison. Within half an hour we bumped into some of the seniors who were more than happy to snitch us in. More order marks were generously granted and we were sent to scrub the tiled floors on our hands and knees in the seniors' accommodation which was in a separate Victorian house up the road.

Something we looked forward to immensely was letters from home. If you were lucky enough to get a food parcel it felt like all your birthdays had come at once. I sometimes would get a parcel from Mum with chocolate, biscuits, and sweets in, though it was against the rules to bring food into the school. If you were unlucky enough to have your birthday during term-time (which I was) it would be like any other day except, in the evening after prep, your year group would gather in the kitchen. There they would sing 'Happy Birthday' and you would be presented with a cake, the cost of which would be added to the bill and sent to your parents.

The meals at school were quite sparse and we were expected to eat what we were given whether we liked it or not and were not allowed to leave the table until it was finished. Breakfast would consist of cereal and a bread roll. Sometimes the bread rolls would be quite stale and cold, but occasionally you could smell the aroma of baked bread and a ripple of excitement would go from one girl to the next. It seemed the cook was feeling generous and had decided to warm the rolls in the oven that day, so even if they were slightly stale the warmth of the oven softened them up. Sometimes though they were left in the oven for too long and they would hard as rocks.

Fridays were my worst days. I detested the breaded fish that would be served up every lunch. It often smelled and tasted slightly rancid. I have never been able to eat breaded fish since, including fish fingers. On Saturdays and Sundays for dinner, each table would be presented with a loaf of bread. This would be duly passed around and we would each take a slice in turn, followed by two spreads. Usually one would consist of 'sandwich spread' which was in a jar with unidentified contents mixed with salad cream, which you would put a dollop of on the side of your plate. For our second course, we would get a piece of Madeira cake and that would be the sum total of dinner. Needless to say, no one had an obesity problem.

However, there was one special bonus on Friday and that was the fruit rationing. We would line up in the evening and each would be handed a banana, two oranges, and an apple. On the way up the stairs to our dormitories, there would be a scurry of activity as we would swap our favourite fruits with each other. I think this was supposed to be part of our five-a-day, which at SMG was five-a-week.

But the best bonus on Fridays was that Miss. Richardson took the evening off. There were two matrons brought in as cover housemistresses. One was called Madame Pompiere, a strict 25-year-old lady of African descent who had a French accent, and another whom we simply called 'Matron'. We preferred this matron because she was lenient with us. She must have liked me for some reason as one day she was having a clear out and gave me a red ball-gown dress which I treasured for many years. It was chiffon with one shoulder strap and a diamante brooch.

The only time we would be able to dress up was for the school Christmas party. We would have a Christmas dinner with the staff and then have a talent show in the hall. One year I was part of a group that put together a short play of the story of the nativity to rock music. Mrs. Cook, the Headmistress, was not amused.

Friday and Saturday evenings we were allowed to watch TV. We would gather in the hall around a tiny TV set whilst sitting on hard plastic blue chairs. We would ensure that the row behind was in between the girls in front so that all could see. It was the era of the Dallas series and we were keen to watch the saga unfold and the latest antics of J R Ewing. The nice matron would often let us stay up later too. Of course, there would be some advantage taken of this relaxation of rules and we would play dares.

There was one girl called Andrea Worley who did not seem to be afraid of anything or anyone. She once threw her teddy at Miss. Richardson – which astonished me at the time. I thought she would surely be excluded for such a vile offence, but Miss. Richardson simply walked out of the room. I do not think she knew how to handle her and must have sensed her lack of fear! At that time I thought Andrea was the bravest person I had ever met. She was always up for a dare and on Friday evenings we would send her up and down the fire escape in the dark and get her to sneak into Mrs. Cook's office.

One such dare went a bit too far. It was harvest festival. Food had been brought in by the day pupils and we had been given a piece of something or a tin to take up to the front during the morning assembly. That night was a Friday. The food had been stored in cardboard boxes along the corridors near our dormitories ready to be taken to who knows where the next day. Someone must have dared Andrea to take something from the box. Then someone else dared someone else and someone else, someone else. Before you knew it pretty much most of it was gone. The lids were put back on the boxes in the hopes that no one would notice.

The next morning as we were all standing by our place at the breakfast table, Miss. Richardson stomped in with her court shoes. It was announced that our mischief had been discovered and a drawer inspection was ordered. Miss. Richardson made her way around the house and eventually stamped into our dorm. I had covered my little stash with a blanket in my under-the-bed drawer. "Lift up the blanket", she said. With trembling hands, I tentatively lifted the blanket hoping that by some miracle they would have disappeared, but there were my stolen goods.

As the majority of us had been involved in the incident they decided to teach us all a lesson and call the police. I cannot imagine what they thought. They must have seen some humour in it, but we were given a serious talk about the fact that stealing was wrong and that stealing one thing, would lead to another which would eventually lead us to jail. I think we had a pretty good idea of what conditions might be like in there. We were all gated for the rest of the term and banned from watching TV.

The headmistress, Mrs. Cook, was another formidable woman. It was easy to remember her age as she had been born in 1900. So whatever year it was, was how old she was. When I arrived at SMG she was 83 and by the time I left she was 88 and she single-handedly ran the school. She looked ancient to me then and walked with a stick. Some of my classmates had been on the receiving end of her stick, Andrea more than once. Corporal punishment was finally made illegal in British schools and children's homes in 1986.

Mrs. Cook had an extraordinary collection of large hats that she wore on Sundays, special events, and sometimes to the morning assembly. There she would play the piano, which would always include several hymns. She would often play off-key which would be an endless source of amusement, much like watching a Les Dawson sketch. She also was known to fall asleep mid hymn when the organ would suddenly land on one key and hold there for a length of time until she woke up and revitalised.

Mrs. Cook was of the Victorian era where girls should be 'seen and not heard'. She did not like any noise at all but luckily was quite hard of hearing. Once she had finished in her office for the day, in which she was often caught taking naps, she would shuffle across the hallway to her bedroom. We then would wait for the additional all-clear, which meant whoever was on watch that night had seen Miss. Richardson's white Lada leave the driveway. This meant that more than 100 girls between the ages of 13 and 16 in the main boarding house had been left in the care of an extremely deaf lady in her eighties, who was fast asleep without her hearing aids in. So we did have some opportunity for fun at last. Midnight feasts were a thing. Though looking back I do not know what the attraction was. Why would anyone hoard a load of food and then scoff it all at the strike of twelve? Nowadays I would end up with indigestion.

At school, you could choose certain out-of-school activities and I chose horse riding. My Auntie Marjorie had taken me a few times to Dicky Steps riding school round the back of Hollingworth Lake in Rochdale when I was younger. I had also learned some riding skills at the Munster Garrison Pony Club in Germany, a riding school that specialised in dressage. A mad goat had lived at the stables and why it was not restrained I will never know. He would constantly charge at us and ram us with his horns whenever he caught us off guard. We walked around constantly scanning our peripheral vision for his appearance and would make a mad dash for it when we were in his view.

Once a week at SMG, friendly old Sid would take us by minibus to West Parley in the New Forest to some riding stables owned by an eccentric lady called Miss Bush, who was also in her eighties. We would go cantering through the woods and over the fields. I was always given a horse called Trigger. I wondered at first why no one else wanted to ride him and why he had that name. I soon found out. For the first and last part of our ride, we would have to go along the main road. Clearly Trigger did not like cars and I would frequently be on the receiving end of him being triggered and running off in all directions, trying to buck me off as he went. Thankfully there were not any serious accidents, but I did come pretty close on several occasions. I recently read some old school letters that stated I had been allowed to lead the hack out and go off alone with another school friend. Maybe this was so they could keep their eye on me and keep me out of other people's harm's way whilst on Trigger.

The school also thought it would be a good idea for me to have elocution lessons, probably trying to drive out my northern accent. I took some exams in 'speaking verse and prose' certified by the London Academy of Music and Dramatic Art. I cannot say they did me any good, my northern accent was here to stay. Yet these activities were a shift in the routine which helped us get through the long weeks and months.

Every evening after dinner we would be ushered into the main hall where tables and hard plastic chairs were laid out much like for exams and we would have 'prep'. A term used for the several hours of homework we would have to do before bed. We would often have Mrs. Cook supervising who would sit at a table on the stage and ensure that there was no talking and that much work was being completed. However, she would often fall asleep. When it would be time to be released we would take it in turns to cough loudly or drop a book on the floor to try and wake her up so we could be dismissed.

Prep was repeated on Saturday mornings from 9 until 12. I was very fortunate to enjoy and have some level of ability for sports. I was on the team for tennis, rounders, netball, and hockey. Being only 270 girls in the whole school meant it was much easier to gain a place on a team as there was much less competition. We rarely won a game as other schools had far more talent to choose from and had much better facilities. However, being on a team meant that you got to escape from Saturday morning prep to play against other schools such as Talbot Heath and Sherbourne in the area.

Swimming took place weekly, a sport I did not enjoy very much at all. I still do not choose to get into cold water, unless I am in at least 90-degree heat. Every

Wednesday we would clamber onto the coach to go to Dolphin's swimming pool. The journey always seemed to be timed with Radio 1's 'Our Tune'. The violin would start and a segment in which a tragic personal story of loss or misery would be read from a listener's letter along with a song that had significance to them. It was certainly something we could have done without at the time. Although looking back we seemed to enjoy it. Maybe it served to help us feel better, reminding us that there are always others worse off in life.

Chapter Six ∞ Breaking Free

I walked into my son's bedroom recently and heard the beginning of an old familiar tune, 'I want to break free', by Queen. My son was on a video call with his friend as they had decided to listen to some golden oldies together. I surprised him by opening the door with a pretend microphone and singing all the words to him. He seemed amused.

It is amazing how a song can instantly transport you back in time. That song took me right back to an SMG school open day in 1984, the year the song was released. We had chosen it as the song to perform a gymnastic routine to. It was a full routine complete with front and back angels, a gymnastic drill that meant you balance another in the air with your feet and at one point it resulted in me standing on the other girl's shoulders. I think the choice of song title may have been subconscious.

Open days were a big deal that we spent weeks preparing for. It was a chance to show what a 'lovely' school SMG was and we would have to try and show how happy we all were. Everything would be scrubbed and polished from floors to windows, to shoes to noses. As Mum was out of the country for some of the years, my Auntie Ellie would come and support me and sometimes take me back to her house for half term.

Lessons were like others in any other school, except they took place in the same building where we slept, ate, and spent all our free time. We would walk up the stairs, passing by our dormitories as we made our way up to the science lab in the loft. The science teacher was called Mr. Balding; he was tall, with an archetypical 'mad professor' hairstyle. You dare not misbehave or you would find the wooden board rubber being launched in your direction. One particular experiment he seemed to really enjoy and repeat often was the electric shock test. He would have us all join hands in a circle and send an electric shock through us all. It probably would be considered a minor shock but nonetheless, I hated the feeling of the jolt riding up one arm and down the other to the next girl. Mr. Balding always stood outside of the circle with what I am sure was a strange smirk upon his face.

However, our PE teacher was very much liked. Her name was Miss. Reed. I think she felt sorry for us all as when with her and away from school, the usual rules seemed to relax. I was fortunate enough to go on a few annual school ski trips which she organised to the Tyrol Valley in Austria. These were times when we felt like we left childhood behind and were treated with individuality and familiarity. On one of the trips, there was a group from a boys' boarding school in the same hotel which added much to the excitement. That year our coach pulled away from the hotel in the early hours of the morning to take us back to the airport. I could see the snow-capped mountains as the sky was getting ready to welcome the morning sun. Just as we were pulling away 'Stand by me' by Ben E King came on the radio and we cried that we were leaving so soon.

Every Sunday we would have to attend church. There were two choices, either St. Katherine's Church of England or Our Lady Queen of Peace, the local Catholic Church. Dad was by now a very ardent Catholic and insisted that each of his children attend mass each week and confession on Saturdays. Confession would often go like this, "Father I have sinned it has been one week since my last confession". The priest would reply, "OK child what have you to confess?" I would then stumble and say something like, "Er I didn't do the washing up when I should've done". I would then wait for the punishment which would invariably be four "hail Marys" and two "our Fathers" and I would go to the altar to kneel and do my penance. The washing up one came up quite a lot, as it would be difficult to think of something on the spot and maybe even at times difficult to be completely honest.

Our Lady's had the benefit of being a strict one-hour-long mass, whereas St. Katherine's could go on much longer. That in itself made it worthwhile being a Catholic. We would all leave on Sunday mornings, whatever the weather, in full dress uniform, in twos, walking in a crocodile procession. Our Lady Queen of Peace was a high Catholic church, so the masses were all in Latin. Although I was doing Latin GCSE at the time, I still did not have a clue what they were saying. I was always mesmerised by the red flickering light near the altar and was told it was the Holy Spirit. I could not quite understand how he had got in there and what he was doing in there. One day I walked away and thought to myself, 'If only church was more relevant for young people, where they played guitars and looked happy'. I had no idea such places existed.

As the years went on Lou and I formed a close bond. We were both quite deep thinkers and would spend hours talking together. One day Lou and I discovered a room in the basement that could be accessed from the front of the building. No one seemed to know about this room, so we would sneak off there and sit and eat Hellas chocolate bars and talk about what the meaning of life might be. Of course, we had no answers then, only lots of questions.

Lou was very much into music and was an avid David Bowie fan. The year we were due to leave school, she also introduced me to the band The Cure and we both decided that we would be vegetarian and wear only black. That phase did not last very long, not while there was a Wimpy in Plymouth.

Our school did not have much land. There was the main house, three portacabin-like buildings that were classrooms, a tennis court, a climbing frame that we called 'the bars', and a certain pine tree that had a big, thick trunk. I have always loved the smell of pine, not the toilet cleaning variety, but the true aroma you experience when standing under a cluster of pine trees. At the front of the school building, there was a large lawn that had to double up as a small rounders field in the summer. On warm evenings we would walk with our best friend, arms linked around a circuit that encircled the tennis court and one of the classrooms. We would walk round and round for hours much like hamsters in a cage on a wheel.

It was amazing the skills that were developed on the climbing bars – you could have signed many of the girls up for a life-long career at the circus there and then. I was not as good as most of them, but I did learn the most common trick. This was to hang from the bars with knees bent and head down and then swing as high as you could with your arms flapping before flipping your legs off and landing on your feet. It is a phenomenon that nobody broke their neck. I found some bars at Tatton Hall Park when my boys were younger and amazed them with this little trick. I still just about had the knack though I would think better of attempting it now.

SMG began as Grassendale School, and by 1914 was 'perhaps better known than any other high-class young ladies school in the United Kingdom', according to a book Mrs. Cook had written. She had taken over the school in 1950 and ran it until she was 87 years old when she suffered a fall and broke her hip. After 102 years of operating, she finally decided to close the school down. Our year was the very first to take GCSEs, before that it had been O Levels, and I along with the other 23 girls in my year were the last to complete our exams before the school closure. I felt sorry for those who, at the last minute, had to find new schools. In all honesty, though, I do not think anyone would have shed a tear about not going back there after the summer. Mrs. Cook died the following year. The building was sold and demolished and sheltered retirement homes were built on the land. It was renamed St. Mary's Court, retaining in part, the name of the old school.

Almost 40 years later, Lou and I rented a holiday house by Southbourne beach and went to the site where the old school had been. As we were staring at the building an elderly lady was coming back from her shopping. We told her that we had been former pupils of the school that had stood on the site and she invited us in for a cup of tea. We went out into the back communal gardens. The tennis court had gone, and so too had the bars. Yet the old pine tree was still there which brought back a flood of memories. That holiday we went to the beach every single day.

For the first two years of my life at SMG, Mum and David lived in Germany where David was stationed. They lived on a street called Sandfortskamp. It was not on a camp at all but was a row of houses that had been contracted to the British Army. Each Christmas, Easter, and Summer I would fly from RAF Hendon or Luton airport to RAF Gutersloh military airbase where I would be picked up to spend my main holidays with them. Germany seemed very neat, clean, and orderly. Summers were spent at the Freibad Coburg, the outdoor swimming pool which was across the road from where we lived. It was here I tasted my first authentic bratwurst, which was sold in the pool café. Winters were cold and would be spent skating on Lake Aasee in the centre of Munster, where immaculately dressed German ladies would walk around in their long fur coats and hats. It was the year Christopher Dean and Jayne Torvill won the gold medal at the Sarajevo Winter Olympics which I was watching at my friend's house one night on a sleepover.

It was on another lake in Germany, the Dummersee, where I first learned to sail. It had been built to host part of the 1936 Olympic Games, has a surface area of 13.5 kilometres and an average depth of one metre. I discovered this a few times whilst sailing when the winds would change and the boom would fly across the boat knocking me on the head and into the water. It was nice to know that however far out from the shore you were that you could simply stand up and climb back into the boat. This was a procedure that was repeated often.

Whenever we wanted a taste of something British, we would visit the nearest NAAFI (the Navy Army Air Force Institute). NAAFI's were established in 1920 by the British Government to run the recreational establishments for all the armed forces to sell 'a taste of home' to servicemen and their families abroad. The things on sale always looked like they had been there for years and the clothes were very old-fashioned. It sold everything from British teabags, washing machines to skis – which is where my first and only pair of cross country skis were purchased.

David's love of skiing was formed from the annual exercise that his troop would carry out in Norway. Every winter he would spend three months there learning all about Arctic warfare. Mum and I took several trips to Norway staying with a family that David had formed a strong friendship with, Marguun and Wiggo (pronounced Viggo) and their two boys. Wiggo owned the village bakery in Dombas where he supplied baked goods to the army and he made the most amazing custard pastries.

In most villages and towns in Norway, there is a local ski slope and I would spend the evening skiing with the village children and then come home to their log-built house with a large open fire. We ate reindeer and cheese for breakfast and there was always four or five feet of snow outside. I marvelled at how meticulously organised they were at clearing the previous night's snowfall from paths and driveways. In Rochdale, if even half a centimetre of snow falls, everyone is tempted to tell work that they are snowed in for fear of skidding. In Norway, they have very tight-knit communities and extended families often live on the same street. They were very welcoming of us, instantly making us feel part of their family and it was fascinating to immerse ourselves into their culture.

In July 1985 David was posted again back to Plymouth. This meant that I could go home for half-term holidays as well as the main holidays. On the way back to SMG after each holiday, we would call in at the Little Chef for my last supper, where I would feast on pancakes and maple syrup. Around this time Bob Geldof launched his 'Feed the World' campaign. The song was recorded in a day and was the fastest-selling single in UK chart history, selling a total of three million copies. That Christmas, I came down to my presents and decided that I would listen to the record and think about the poor people in Africa before I would touch any of them. It seemed a very noble action at the time and stopped me from feeling as guilty for opening up my presents and eating my Christmas dinner.

Chapter Seven ∞ Italian Reunions

I walked into the spare bedroom of our army quarter in Plymouth and found Nana, who had been visiting with us, on the floor making strange noises. Her mouth had drooped on one side, she could not speak and I could not get her up. I was 14 years old and alone with her and I knew something was very wrong. I ran to the neighbour's house to use the phone and an ambulance was called for. Nana was admitted to Derriford Hospital where she spent two weeks recovering from a stroke that had affected the right side of her body. After that she struggled to speak and when she did it sounded like she was speaking Italian. She was 62 years old.

Five years later we decided to take a road trip and take her back to see her relatives in Italy, we also wanted to know if they could understand what she was saying. She had only been back once in the 41 years since she had arrived in England. She felt, like many others who had left, that she could not return unless she had made something of herself.

Nana remained a mill girl for her whole working life, ending up working at Minky Mill on John Street in Rochdale. It produced an assortment of household products such as ironing board covers and tea towels. Nana ran the machine that rolled stockinette cloth into rolls to be later hemmed and cut into dishcloths. She loved working there, had many friends, and wholeheartedly joined in the work's Christmas parties. It is still there to this day and I sometimes glance at the doorway where we used to wait for her to finish work more than three decades ago.

Prior to our trip to Italy, Mum and David had just bought a brand new champagne-coloured Nissan Bluebird. It seemed incredibly flash at the time and it had electric windows which I had never seen before. The interior was cream velour and it had a sunroof. The four of us hit the road travelling through France, Switzerland, and the Saint Bernadino Tunnel into Italy. Nana resisted giving up her smoking habit, even after the stroke and I remember David being mad as ever as she burned three cigarette holes in the ceiling of the new car whilst we were travelling.

That trip to Italy in 1991 was magical. We arrived in Baranello, in the province of Campobasso, and it looked like it had been untouched since Nana had left in 1950. It is still a small village today with a population of around 2,600 people, but even then it was far smaller. It is a farming community mainly producing beans, grapes, olives, and durum wheat. Nana was hoping to catch her brother, Pasquale whom she had not seen for over 40 years. He and his wife Carmella had been visiting family and were due to fly back home that day to Brisbane where they lived in Australia. Thankfully the flight ended up being much later than we thought and they were able to see each other.

We started by first looking for Nana's aunt, her mother's sister whom we had been told was still alive. As we walked up the steep, cobbled street we saw a little old lady dressed in black on a balcony. We had been taught to ask "Dove abita Angelina Giovaniti" (where does Angelina Giovaniti live?) and she directed us to the other side of the village. As we drove a little while on, Nana banged her hands on the car headrest in front and shouted, "Basta, basta". David assumed that meant 'stop the car' and not that she was calling him a name. She opened the car door and made her way to a house and started banging on an old wooden door. There she found Auntie Angelina whom she had not seen for decades. Later Angelina's husband walked us around the village and showed us the house where Nana had grown up, and my great-grandfather's blacksmith shop. Strangely my great-grandfather on Mum's father's side of the family had also been a blacksmith.

We also went into the church of Saint Michael Archangel (or San Michele Arcangelo) which Nana had attended throughout her childhood. In the church are some frescoes that one of my great-grandmother's cousins, Amedeo Trivisonno, had painted. Amedeo Trivisonno was born in Campobasso in 1904 and had studied painting at the Academy of Rome. He was attracted to the Renaissance and was also interested in the anatomy of the human body. He spent hours in the operating rooms of the morgue attending autopsies whilst taking chemistry lessons to understand the subject better. Amedeo was fascinated by the fresco technique and was frequently seen painting frescoes on empty white walls of houses under construction. He kept a diary which later became his 'Memoirs', an autobiography in verse that was published in 1989.

At the age of 22 years old, Amedeo began painting frescoes in churches beginning with the story of Saint Nicholas of Bari in Abruzzo. It was this Nicholas who had a reputation for giving gifts in secret. He was known for many acts of benevolence; those in need would place their shoes out and under the cover of night Nicholas would put gold coins in them. From these acts the tradition of Santa Claus evolved. In 1930 Amedeo moved to Rome and opened a studio in Piazza Dante. During the Second World War, Amedeo painted many portraits of Canadian, American, and British soldiers who had been sent to convalesce in Campobasso. Before leaving for the frontline, they would collect their portraits and would send them sent back home to their families. Only one painting had not been collected, it was a portrait of a British soldier.

On 18th November 1969, Amedeo's daughter, Anna Maria, placed an advert in the Daily Telegraph in London of this painting to promote his artwork abroad. Less than one month later news arrived home in Florence, where they then lived, that the soldier in the painting had been found. He had recognised himself in the portrait and contacted Amedeo's family. Not long after he came with his wife and daughter to claim the painting which started a beautiful friendship. This led other ex-soldiers to Florence to find Amedeo Trivisonno and talk about the old days.

Amedeo was very devoted to the Christian faith. He married Maria Rosaria in 1927 and together they had 12 children. He was later commissioned by Bishop Romita to work on the frescoes of the Cathedral in Campobasso which depict stories from the Old and New Testament on over 150 meters of wall. Amedeo also devoted himself to composing sacred music and gave lectures on Bach and Chopin. He would say to his daughters, "Painting is like music, it has the same language, one pleases the eye, the other the ear".

His works are all monumental, from the fresco in Campobasso to the 'Last Supper' at Colle d'Anchise measuring 72 square meters. In this, Christ and the Apostles occupy the centre of the painting. All around, enveloped in a nebula that emphasises the distance in time between the various characters, God Himself stands in the centre surrounded by the Universe and hosts of angels. Lower down in the painting are the prophets, Abraham, Melchizedek, and ancient nomads of the desert. His art can also be seen in the Basilica Minore dell'Addolorata di Castelpetroso, where he paints eight large canvases. For these canvases, the models were family members and often the villagers with their faces looking tired but authentic.

Amedeo Trivisonno was a Master in the true sense of the word, passing on everything he knew to others including students and children. He suffered greatly from the premature death of his son who died at the age of 38 and he himself died in Florence in 1995. Over his lifetime he created over 4,500 square meters of frescoes in 45 churches in five different Italian regions and also one in Cairo, Egypt. It is on my bucket list to one day tour Italy visiting all the churches in which Amedeo left his mark.

His daughter, Maria Trivisonno, is also an artist in her own right, and I met her at my cousin Tom's wedding in 2014. The reception was held at the Villa Richter in Prague in the Czech Republic which has the most spectacular panoramic view of the city.

One abiding memory of that day is that whilst the adults were all busy chatting, the younger boys of the wedding party, including my own, decided to slide down a steep, grassy verge in a neighbouring vineyard in their wedding suits. A man, who looked much like a gardener, appeared with arms flapping, shouting loudly at them in Czech. I have discovered since that this vineyard belonged to Saint Wenceslas and had its beginnings in the 10th century. According to the legend, it is one of the oldest vineyards in Bohemia, where it was cared for by Saint Wenceslas, the patron of the Bohemian Lands. The renovated vineyard has grape varieties of Pinot Noir and Rhine Riesling. No wonder the gardener was a little upset and those stains never did come out of their suits.

We all know the Christmas carol, 'Good King Wenceslas', who last looked out on the feast of Steven, when the snow was deep and crisp and even. It tells the story of a Bohemian king who lived during the years 907–935. He was known to have braved the harsh winter weather to give alms to a poor peasant on the Feast of Stephen (26th December). During the journey, his aide is about to give up but is enabled to continue by following the king's footprints, step for step, through the deep snow.

The tale is based on the life of the real historical figure of Saint Wenceslas I, Duke of Bohemia (an area now part of the Czech Republic). He stood for Christian values amid political unrest. He was known to rise barefoot from his bed each night to give alms generously to widows, orphans, those in prison, and those afflicted by every difficulty, so much so that he was considered the father of all the poor. His saintly grandmother, Ludmilla, raised him and promoted him as ruler of Bohemia in place of his mother, who upheld anti-Christian beliefs. Ludmilla was ultimately murdered, but rival Christian forces enabled Wenceslas to assume leadership of the government.

Wenceslas' influence facilitated unity within Bohemia and created peace-making negotiations with Germany, which caused him trouble with the anti-Christian opposition. His brother, Boleslav, who opposed him, eventually led him to his death, and Wenceslas was hailed as a martyr with his tomb becoming a pilgrimage destination. He is now hailed as the patron of the former Czechoslovakia and the Bohemian people.

My cousin, Tom, was born twenty years later than Michael and me and was ten years old when he emigrated to Australia with my auntie and uncle. When he was in his early twenties he went travelling around Europe and met his future bride in Prague. We have visited a few times, once to attend their first baby's baptism. It was December and Wenceslas' square was filled with snow-topped Christmas market stalls, where we drank hot chocolate in a café that claims to be where it was first produced in Europe.

I digress... back to our trip to Italy in 1991, a huge, long table was spread out on a rooftop terrace in Nana's village of Baranello, which was soon filled with extended family members all chattering away loudly in Italian. We were served courses of pasta, meats, salads, and desserts. Pasquale sat with Nana, his sister, catching up after over 40 lost years. 15 years later I was able to connect with Pasquale and Carmella and their grownup children Tony and Michael when I took my own three boys to Australia a couple of times. It was wonderful to meet the Italian side of my family for the first time; cousins, aunties, and uncles. Whilst in Italy we stayed at the home of Nana's other brother, Ugo who had sadly passed away in April just a few months before we arrived. Ugo had a son called Elvio, who was around the same age as me, so he showed me around.

Nana had three other siblings; there was Irma, who lived in an apartment in Paris, and also Guiseppe, known as Peppino. Peppino had left Italy in his early twenties and was never seen again. Rumour has it that he was trapped in East Germany when the Berlin wall was erected on the night of the 12th of August 1961. He had allegedly been shot trying to cross back over into West Germany.

Ugo had owned a fruit and veg shop in Campobasso, the main town eight miles away from Baranello. It was on a corner and had the 'Frutta e Verdura' sign above the door. He had also been a market stallholder and on market days would set up a stall selling kitchen equipment. It was now up to Elvio and his soon-to-be bride, Guilliana, to carry on the family business. I went with them to market one day and helped set up. There were more pots and pans on that stall than a whole village could use in a lifetime. I could not believe how much effort it took to unpack and repack them all painstakingly into the back of a van at the beginning and end of every market day.

Nana's other sister Concetta (pronounced 'Conchetta') lived, like many in Italy, in a modern apartment block with her husband Dante and their two girls Elisabetta and Mara. They had moved 200 miles away to Ancona which is situated on the Adriatic Sea and is famous for its white picturesque beaches at the base of Mount Conero. It is off the tourist map and is mostly known as a modern port, but it also has an appealing historic town on a hill. Though we could not speak Italian and they could not speak much English we muddled through using sign language and phrasebooks. There was no Google translate in those days. Mara had just bought her first car and she would whizz me around the streets of Ancona like she was in the Italian Grand Prix.

Mara was the one to introduce me to a game where you wave at passers-by. She would say to me in pigeon English, 'Look how stupid Italians are', I think she used the word 'loco'. She would see someone walking on the pavement, beep her horn and wave her arms wildly. The poor unsuspecting pedestrian, presuming it was some friend or other would enthusiastically wave back. We would be in fits of laughter. I have since played the game in England; it seems we are just as loco over here. My boys got me to do it the other day, but I do feel a little guilty now for laughing at someone else's expense. I don't play it very often. My son (my 18 year old) said, "But Mum, it brightens up someone's day making them think someone cares for them". I don't think that justifies it somehow.

In 1988 David was making his exit out of the army and was considering what to do next. Mum's best friend Linda worked in a care home and suggested both couples open and run a care home together. The search was on for the right property, the Griffins looking in Rochdale and Mum and David looking in Plymouth. It was decided that whichever family found the right property at the right price, the other family would relocate. Along the same road where Linda and Griff lived on Milkstone Road was Zion Baptist Church. The church owned an old large house that was being used as their youth centre, it was for sale and going cheap. At the time Mum saw no other option than for us to move back to Rochdale. We cried all the way up the M6 and she vowed it would only be for a few years and then we would return to the city of Plymouth which we had come to love. That was in 1988 and we are still here, though I did manage to escape Rochdale for a while. Though I have come to realise there are far worse places to live in the world.

The property was purchased and a builder sourced to carry out the necessary renovations. By then Mum and David had bought and renovated a lovely house in Crownhill in Plymouth called Maker View. They decided to rent the house out to ensure we had a reason to go back and we moved into a flat above the care home. David had been posted to Catterick barracks in Richmond, North Yorkshire to complete his army service. When my GCSE results came through I was pleased to discover I passed all nine of them with reasonable results, the whole SMG experience had fulfilled its ultimate purpose. Mum then enrolled me at Bury Grammar school, a private day school for Girls. It was the last thing I wanted.

That first morning at Bury Grammar we were ushered into the assembly hall. The headmistress walked onto the stage with a cap and gown on and I knew I had to get out of there fast. After being restricted for most of my teenage years I had every intention of living it up and no intention of studying. I also knew how expensive the school was and knew that I would just be throwing Mum's money down the drain. At this school, I met a friend called Sonya. She had been there for most of her school life and felt that she too needed to get out. Unbeknown to our parents, we made a pact together that we would go to the headmistress' office and tell her of our intention to leave the school.

Dad seemed to take charge at this time and went to speak to the local Catholic Sixth Form College across the road from where he lived on Manchester Road in Bury, called Holy Cross. Some distant aunt or other had been a Nun there in the past which seemed to swing it for me to enrol even though the college year was already underway. It was not the total freedom I was looking for but it felt less restrictive than Bury Grammar and there were no fees, so I was not going to waste anyone's money. Meanwhile, Sonya went to study law at the local college and went on to become a successful partner in a solicitor's firm.

I was right; I was in no mood for working hard at college. I passed my driving test and got my first car, a dark red Volkswagen Derby. Instead of attending lessons a few of us would pile into my car and we would go up to

Pilsworth Industrial Estate where there was a new Asda with a café. My friend smoked and though I tried it, it held no appeal. Maybe seeing Nana suffer from her stroke and the cigarette burns in the car roof had put me off.

It was on the Pilsworth Trading Estate in Bury that I got my first weekend job. A new Warner Brothers cinema had opened and they were looking for staff. I received my crisp, new royal blue uniform and set off for work feeling rather smart. There was a big launch event and Liza Minnelli was cutting the ribbon. I cannot say I knew who she was, Dad pursed his lips when I told him, he clearly knew. However, I did know who Kevin and Sally Webster were from Coronation Street who came up to me for some orange juice that I was holding out on a silver tray. Being a northern girl I had been fed a steady diet of 'the Street' growing up, so I was a little star-struck.

My friends appreciated my new job. Sonya had introduced me to a group of lads she had been hanging out with for many years. When I was not at work at the weekends we would be in our corner of Madison's pub in Rochdale. When I was at work I would be tiptoeing down a plush carpeted corridor to the fire escape and letting them sneak in to watch the films for free. There cannot have been many CCTV cameras in those days.

At Holy Cross I was studying for a social biology A level which involved a field trip in the Lake District, staying at a youth hostel, the YHA in Langdale. The boys decided to come too and followed the school minibus all the way to Ambleside. My Biology teacher, Mr. Gartside said, "Joanne will you please tell your friends to stop following us". That evening they sneaked into our room at the Youth Hostel. When it was found that someone was coming down the corridor they each jumped out of the second-floor window onto the grass below. I am amazed none of them broke any legs. Mr. Gartside was not impressed; though he hardly had a leg to stand on as he went on to marry one of our classmates. She was always the first to arrive for the lesson and always the last to leave.

Sonya was the unfortunate passenger of my only serious car crash. I had not been driving long when I was travelling down Albert Royds Street late at night behind a slow-moving truck. I started to pull out to overtake and sped up, but misjudged it and hit the bollard on the central reservation. I vaguely recall seeing the bollard flying up into the air, smashing into about a hundred pieces. As we careened to the left-hand side of the road I found that my front, right wheel had been shunted 90 degrees. We must have missed the centre lamppost by millimetres – it was a close call. My Volkswagen Derby was no more and if I had hit the lamppost we might not be here either.

At that time Sonya was working weekends at the Bellavista restaurant on Wildhouse Lane in Milnrow. Later, she managed to get me a job there and I worked behind the bar. I enjoyed talking with the regulars and would make some good tips. Sergio, the owner, had quite a few good restaurants around Greater Manchester and was trying to get his children interested in the family business. His son and I were the same age and often worked the bar together. At that time he had little interest in the restaurant trade, but he now manages the San Rocco in

Ashton. Before the doors would open every evening the chefs would make us all dinner and we would all sit around and eat together. It very much reminded me of that time in Italy on the roof terrace. If we were hungry later in the evening we would nip into the kitchen and make ourselves Parma ham sandwiches on thick crusty bread. For many years we would take Nana to the Bellavista for her birthday lunch on the 23rd of September. We still choose to go to the Bellavista now for family occasions and a few of the staff still work there some thirty years later.

At Holy Cross, I met another new friend called Adelle Rakin. She was a cross country running champion and spent many weekends at some race or other, but Thursday, Friday and Saturday nights were going out nights. We would start at Madison's pub then end up in Bentley's, a small nightclub in Rochdale. There I would often bump into my Uncle Mick, Mum's brother, and his partner, who seemed to be well known around town. I felt like I had some kudos from being his niece and we would often be able to bypass the lines to get into the clubs. Adelle ended up winning a running scholarship at Michigan University and off she went to study in America.

In 1989 my Auntie Ellie and Uncle Andrew were taking a trip to California to visit relatives and were kind enough to invite me. I was 18 years old and keen to meet my extended family and experience America – 'the land of the free and the home of the brave'. This was the first time I met Siobhan, a first cousin of Mum and Auntie Ellie. We were closer in age than she was to them and we became close, life-long friends. We stayed with Siobhan and her husband, Mark in Carlsbad, visiting San Diego and the theme parks of Los Angeles.

One day we took a day trip crossing the border into Tijuana, Mexico where I bought a pair of cowboy boots from one of the astonishing number of shops and market stalls. On October 17th we decided to take a trip further north to San Francisco to do some sightseeing. We were approaching the San Luis Obispo area on the US-101 N when a 6.9 magnitude earthquake hit the San Francisco Bay Area lasting around 60 seconds. 67 people died and a further 3,000 others were injured. It caused over $5 billion worth of damage. The centre of the quake was near the Loma Prieta Peak in the Santa Cruz Mountains which was around 150 miles north and on route to where we were heading. Had the earthquake hit 24 hours later we would probably have been in the Bay Area visiting Fisherman's Wharf, the area which had been most devastated. Interestingly here is another link back to Rochdale, the man who invented the seismograph that measures earthquakes was John Milne, a British geologist and mining engineer who was raised in Milnrow in Rochdale. There is a pub there now named after him.

After completing college, I started to work the night shift as a care assistant at our Care Home. One of my co-workers was Brenda Hill, a fun-loving girl who had been through a lot in life but had such an upbeat, positive attitude. She attended Zion church across the road. To try and keep awake we would have KEY 103 radio on in the dining room. When we could not take it any longer we would get the cushions from the lounge and make a little bed under the nurse call system and take turns to have a nap. I was thankful I only lived upstairs and would crawl up to bed once the day staff came on.

There were only 15 residents then and I was living in the same house, so they all soon felt like extra Grandparents to me. One evening whilst on shift, I was cleaning up after a night-time accident from one of the residents and had a Eureka moment. Did I want to be doing this for the rest of my life? Not that it is a futile job, it is not, but I felt that I wanted to do so much more with my life. It was then that I started to think about higher education.

My eyes look round as I reflect,
I try to think and recollect
That slowly moving rocking chair,
in which she sat so quietly there.
A sad old lady, timid and frail,
her crinkled face so deathly pale.
But I recall one winter's night,
when from her face so clear and bright
There came a warm and radiant smile,
that seemed to linger just awhile
As she remembered times long past,
of love and joy that couldn't last.
And then I'd see the picture change,
she'd look so distant, somewhat strange.
The sadness in her eyes, the tears,
came trickling down through all the years
She'd been alone without a friend.
A tragic life when would it end?
With husband, son and daughter gone,
she had no strength to carry on.
But soon that smile returned,
for then, she knew they'd be together again - AF.

Chapter Eight ∞ Student Days and Corporate Ways

I looked down at the results paper and a wave of disappointment rolled over me. I had not passed one single A level from my two years studying at Holy Cross. Though I had to be honest with myself, I had spent hardly any time studying, instead, I had been driving around in my car and hanging out with friends. However I was interested in doing business studies and as Holy Cross had not offered this, I had previously enrolled at Bury College night school. For this, I got a D. Not an outstanding mark but it was enough to gain me entry at Slough College in Berkshire to do a Business Studies Higher National Diploma (HND). They must have been really desperate to fill their spaces.

And so I left home, not for the first time. I got the accommodation list and managed to secure the spare room of a woman called Pat Turner. She lived in a semi-detached house on Blenheim Road in the Langley area of Slough. It had a long garden with a view of Windsor Castle in the distance. Slough is on the outskirts of the M25 and a short drive away from Heathrow airport. At the same time each day Concorde could be seen flying over our house, though you could hear it before you could see it. It travelled at twice the speed of sound and its fastest crossing from Heathrow to New York was just 2 hours, 52 minutes, and 59 seconds. However, due to rising costs is ceased operating in 2003. It also suffered a huge blow when one of its jets crashed just after take-off in Paris on the 25th of July 2000, killing 109 passengers and crew on board as well as four people on the ground.

Incidentally a cotton-loom machine from Littleborough, Rochdale had been converted to weave fibreglass after the decline of the cotton industry. It was this that went on to produce the moulds that were used to make the Concorde aeroplanes' nose cones. Again another aspect of my story that links back to Rochdale

Pat lived two miles from the college and I would don my desert boots and woollen jumper and set off from Pat's house complete with my headphones and Walkman, (by then the CD Walkman had been invented). Pat lived alone and worked as an Usher at Slough Magistrates Court and as a result, she knew a lot of the local police force. She was known for her baking and there would be a steady stream of on-duty policemen calling in for a brew and a rock cake.

It was not long before I had a group of friends: Katrina, Sarah, Lindsey, Martel, Kevin, and Dominic. We hung out together and had a corner of the study section of the library that we would meet in. We all seemed determined to work hard. I think this was particularly spurred on by Katrina who was slightly older than us. She was very ambitious and had set her face like flint to succeed on the course and in life. She did too, and at one point was the overall Marketing and Customer Experience Manager for Costa Coffee, making all the decisions about what food is on offer in all their outlets. Maybe without her, we would have all floundered somewhat.

Lindsey lived in a big house in Windsor with her father. He owned a company that made machines that sealed up tea bags. If that cannot do well in England I do not know what can. She drove around in a big black Audi which was one of her father's old company cars. Occasionally we would all pile in and go to the iconic Ronnie Scott's Jazz Bar in Soho in London. Though why I do not know as none of us even liked Jazz, I think it was just the thing to do. It was a club that opened in 1959 and over the years had hosted some of the biggest names in the Jazz scene. We would also often go into Windsor to do a bit of shopping or go for a stroll along the river. We would keep an eye out for the Queen in her headscarf and sunglasses disguise, but we never did see her there.

The HND course was two years long or three years with a work placement in the middle. It was the early 90s and Britain was in a recession. The college placement officer basically said there was no one taking on students so if we wanted a work placement we would have to find one ourselves. Coming to the conclusion that it would look better on our CVs if we had some work experience we decided to look around. Katrina found a role in marketing and Sarah in accounts.

Around this time I was sitting in a restaurant pondering what I should do. I looked to the ceiling above my table and there pinned directly above me was a full-size flag of Texas. By now Mark and Siobhan were living in Houston, Texas so I contacted them to look into the idea of living with them. Her husband, Mark, worked in management for the stock brokerage division of American

Express. I asked if he could find me a job there and that following summer found myself on a Continental airline heading for Houston. Texas is known as the lone star state from its lone star flag which was adopted when it became independent from Mexico in 1836. The flag represents the pride of the people and the go-it-alone spirit that is part of the Texas way of life. It is known for its rodeos, chilli cook-offs, and corn dogs, all of which I got to sample. The houses there all seemed enormous compared to the little terraced houses around Rochdale and I had a bedroom with a walk-in wardrobe. Mark found me a job working for Shearson Lehman Brothers in downtown Houston. I passed the Texas driving test and bought a red Toyota car which I would drive to the park and ride and then take a commuter bus into the city.

One day when as I was out driving, my car spluttered and broke down. I had arrived in the US with a set amount of money to be able to buy a car and pay my living expenses until my first paycheque. I was on my own in a foreign city with no mobile phone. When I looked up I realised I had broken down right in front of a car repair garage. I simply got out of the car and walked in and gave them the keys and asked if they could take a look at it and I used the garage phone to ring Siobhan to pick me up. When we got home and I totted up how much money I had. I still remember the grand total came to $103.15. The next day I got a call from the garage, he told me what was wrong with the car and I tentatively asked how much it was going to cost to repair. His reply was $103.15 cents.

To the exact cent that I had to my name. That was a memorable day.

I worked on the 17th floor of a skyscraper in downtown Houston in something called 'the cage', a secured area within the main office. My job was to learn the ropes from a long-standing employee called Rick. He taught me how to process all the transactions from deals made by the stockbrokers, ensuring all the necessary forms were completed accurately. We also had to observe patterns of trading to ensure that all the brokers were working legally and according to company policy. One day I noticed that Rick's tickly cough was worsening as time was going on. He then went off on sick and just two weeks later it was announced, in hushed tones, that he had died of AIDS. By 1994 AIDS was the leading cause of death among all Americans aged between 25 and 44. It was the first time I had come into such close contact with someone with it and watched how quickly it could take a life away.

When I was not at work, I often took care of Siobhan's three boys then aged between 2 and 8 years old. Mark and Siobhan would go on corporate weekend away trips and I would be left with Siobhan's huge black 8-seater Chevrolet station wagon and the boys. We had a lot of fun and I became very fond of each of them. Later I would have my own three boys, so it was an excellent training ground. I also volunteered at the local radio station called KSBJ. I always had an interest in radio and saw the potential of being able to reach people who often feel lost and alone. I took calls on the counselling phone-in line, often just to lend a listening ear to people late at night and to try and impart some hope that things can get better.

The weather always seemed extreme in Houston. The summer heat is intense and storms electrifying to watch. I was driving back from the KSBJ studios one day when I got caught up in a thunderstorm. The rain was coming down so hard there was nothing I could do but stop the car where I was in the middle of the road and wait. The water was creeping up from the ground around the car and lightning coming down at a frightening rate. Thankfully the storm passed over but I had to drive through some fairly deep waters to make my way home.

One day Mark came home with the news that he had been promoted and transferred to New York City. The family was going to have to move. They gave me a choice, did I want to stay there and live with friends, namely one called Renee Summers who I had got close to, or did I want to move. I decided to make the move. A new first-class-only airline had just launched and we managed to get an early discount price to be among the first passengers. So we took off from Houston Airport and once in the sky were given our dinner on silver trays. The three boys were all strapped into their seats behind us. We heard Mickey, the youngest say, "hmm this cheese is nice Mommy". As we turned around he was popping the neatly rolled up butter balls into his mouth one by one. It was definitely a novel experience for us all.

We moved to Middletown, New Jersey, a one-hour drive away from Manhattan, New York. That winter on the 13th March, the 'storm of the century' hit New York and the surrounding states. It later became known as the 'Blizzard of 93' or 'Superstorm '93' and 310 people were killed. We woke up one morning and everything looked frozen in time. Snow had fallen in the early hours which changed to sleet and then quickly to rain. But as the rain fell it turned to ice. The icicles were enormous hanging from every conceivable tree and structure. We had to hunker down until it thawed.

When we arrived in New Jersey I registered with an agency and soon found work as a PA to a New Yorker called David Serena who managed the over-the-counter (OTC) stock brokerage division of Lehman Brothers. In the financial crisis of 2008, Lehman Brothers would make headline news as helping cause the world's worst financial collapse. It went bust as a result of the housing crisis and subsequently caused a loss of over six million jobs.

Back then in 1993 jobs seemed to be two a penny and the New York corporate world was buzzing. Our floor in the American Express Tower in downtown Manhattan consisted of a sea of computer desks with brokers staring at a mass of figures on screens. Minutes before the stock market would open there would be relative calm, then the second it did, there would be a cacophony of people clutching their spiral corded phones, sometimes standing up, sometimes sitting down – all of them trying to maximise their client's portfolios.

My job was to keep the boss happy. He would frequently send me out on errands, which I did not mind as just to be walking the streets of New York as a 22-year-old felt like I was living a dream. I was an Englishwoman in

New York (the song 'Englishman in New York' by Sting had come out six years earlier in 1987). Again I commuted via the park and ride scheme. The bus would drop me off on West Broadway and I would walk through the concourse of the World Trade Center to get to 200 Vesey Street where my building was located. The American Express Tower is a 739-foot skyscraper in Lower Manhattan, the tallest of the three towers that makes up the World Financial Center. The centre is all connected via a glass and steel public space with palm trees from the Mojave Desert, a 20 million-acre desert spanning California, Nevada, Utah, and Arizona.

My two co-workers were Francine and Patti and through the window nearest to us we could see the base of one of the Twin Towers directly across the road from us. The Twin Towers had been built between 1966 and 1975 for the purpose of stimulating urban renewal in Lower Manhattan. The build cost was the equivalent of £1.64 billion today. I still have the souvenir guide of the Towers and the complex.

Beneath the Twin Towers complex was an underground shopping mall, the biggest in New York City imaginatively named the 'Mall at the World Trade Center'. I would often be sent to pick things up such as my boss's glasses from the opticians or lunch from a particular place and would descend down into it from the World Trade Center lobby. Sometimes I would be sent to collect documents from offices in the Twin Towers themselves and other times I undertook general office administration. On the 107th floor of the South Tower of the Twin Towers, there was a public observation deck called 'Top of the World'. I would take visitors up there to see the view of Manhattan and beyond. It was unnerving being up there and astonishing to me that mere man could build something so colossal.

It seemed that corporate money was in abundance back then. We had a choice of lunch each day which was delivered to our desk from the Marriott Hotel, paid for by the company. The stock market does not take a lunch break so neither could we. There was a 'work hard, play hard' ethos. You could take a week off work once you had worked a full six months with no sick days and you then had to work the next six months for another week off. We would often go out for a drink after work or have a late meeting conveniently located in a restaurant in Manhattan and my boss would order me a 'car' to take me the one-hour drive home. It would be a black sedan car with a privately hired driver. I loved the corporate world, wearing business suits and fitting in with the humdrum of business life.

In the February of that year, a terrorist attack had been carried out in the basement of the North Tower of the World Trade Center when a truck bomb was detonated. It was intended to send the North Tower crashing into the South Tower killing tens of thousands of people. It failed then, but little did we know what was to occur eight years later on the 11th of September 2001. I sometimes wonder if any of my co-workers were caught up in that devastating day when 2,606 people lost their lives.

The time had come to move on. I had another year of my business studies to complete back in Slough, England. My boss did offer to get me a visa to stay on and work for him permanently. It was a flattering proposal, but I knew it was time to go. I had another two months before I had to be back to finish my studies and I had accepted the invitation of a trip to South America. Mark Twain once said, "Twenty years from now you will be more disappointed by the things you did not do, so throw off the bowlines, sail away from the safe harbour and catch the trade winds in your sails". I had been invited to stay with another cousin of Mum's who had just moved with his family to Quito, Ecuador.

Quito was another world again. Situated high in the Andes Mountains it sits 9,350 feet above sea level. It is the capital of Ecuador and the second-highest capital city in the world, and the closest city to the equator. It takes quite a few days for your lungs to adjust to the altitude, at first it feels like you cannot breathe. Michael had just got a position as a teacher in the local seminary. They had only been there themselves for a few weeks, so we were all grappling with the Spanish language and Ecuadorian culture.

I found a job on the English desk of a local radio station called HCJB. It was known as 'the voice of the Andes' and had been set up in 1931 to send hope to the multitudes living throughout South America and beyond. Staff members at the station produced their own original radio programming in both Spanish and English and I was often asked to do a voiceover for voice-clips to be aired on the radio. I also opened and responded to all the letters that came through in English. There I also met an English girl who became a good friend.

Living with Michael and Denise was a wonderful experience. I have never seen a couple who I could better term as 'soul mates', so completely devoted to one another and to their children. They were together on a mission to bring hope and do good to the people of Quito. Denise was a fantastic chef and what she did not know about cooking was simply not worth knowing. We would visit the market in Quito together and I would often be in the kitchen as she taught me various dishes. She excelled in hosting dinners and though they had rented only a small apartment, we seemed to have a train of people coming and going sampling Denise's cooking. The weather in Quito has a fairly constant climate and an average temperature of 21.4 °C. Every day is like a nice summer's day in England. We had a motto that we would say to each other every day, "Just another beautiful day in Quito."

In order to get to know the locals, Michael and I used to get up at five in the morning and go to the local park to play tennis where there were several tennis courts. There seemed to be quite a few other crazies up at this hour also playing tennis and we soon made some good friends. One memorable friendship was with an American man named Victor Hugo who had lived in Quito for many years. He owned two hair and beauty salons in Quito and seemed to be quite the local celebrity. We would pop in to see him in the salon and he was always thrilled to see us. The people of South America are so warm and inviting. At the time he was putting a TV commercial together for his business to air on Ecuadorian TV and asked if I would do the voice-over for that too. My northern accent did not seem to matter too much over there.

A few times we took the 16-mile bus ride to La Mitidad Del Mundo – or the city at the middle of the world. It has a monument there to mark the equator and a large market selling blankets, ponchos, jewellery, instruments, and leather goods. The bus rides always felt like you were taking your life into your own hands. Roads often followed cliff drops and people would jam onto the bus, sometimes clutching live chickens. Local Latino music would be blasting through the speakers and the buses looked like they were held together with masking tape and string. They frequently broke down and in the likely event that they did, everyone knew the drill, we all had to get off and push from the rear of the bus and try to dislodge it from whatever pothole it had found itself in.

One day Michael wanted to go and visit one of his students, Pablo, in a very remote village. We all decided to go with him. As we approached by car, the village children all ran out and stared at us. It was clear that a car was not a common sight. Donkeys still trod down the wheat from the fields and children were in scruffy traditional style dress with no shoes on their feet. We spent the day with a family in the village who treated us like privileged guests. It was their custom to serve visitors only the best and so they went off to the guinea pig pen to select one for lunch. Sitting of a bottle crate as a chair in a makeshift kitchen I was given a bowl of thin, yellow-looking soup with a guinea pig leg sticking out of the bowl – much like a chicken leg but with claws on the end. I tried my best to drink the soup and look like I was about to eat the leg as I did not want to offend, but when no one was looking I slung it into Pablo's bowl. He had become a good friend and he just laughed at me and graciously ate it and seemed to enjoy it. Maybe it tastes like chicken, but it was not something I wanted to find out.

Another day we went on a group trip with the students to walk up the snow-capped Cotopaxi Mountain, 30 miles south of Quito. It is the second-highest summit in Ecuador reaching 19,347 feet and is an active volcano. It has had 87 known eruptions since 1534, some quite major and there are approximately 300,000 people known to be at risk from its fallout. The last major eruption lasted from August 2015 until January 2016 and Cotopaxi was officially closed by the authorities for climbers until it was reopened on the 7th October 2017. I had not packed winter clothing so had to borrow a padded coat, a hat, and gloves from the other students. Thinking I was in reasonably good shape I figured that it would not be too difficult to keep up with the group. The ground is covered with volcanic dust, which feels like you have to make three strides for every one.

In 1971, the year I was born, the Jose F Ribas Refuge was built at an elevation of 4,864 feet. The air is so thin I just about made it to the refuge and thought I would pass out if I went any further. Typically of those attempting to reach the summit only about half make it. Maybe I did not do so badly after all, though some in our group went much further. I told them I would wait for them and collapsed to recuperate ready for the descent.

Whilst in Quito I met a woman called Debbie who was living there with her family as a missionary. She asked if I would go with her to visit an American girl in the local prison as we were similar in age. I agreed. We took the bus ride to the Carcel de Mujeres – the women's prison and passed through security. What I saw I will never forget. There were crowds of women and children in the prison and I saw rats openly running up and down the filthy walkways. I met American-born Peggy, which strangely enough was my paternal grandma's name. She was also a spitting image of Lou Moogan so as soon as I met her she felt really familiar, which often happens when someone resembles someone else you have known.

The authorities had allowed Peggy to have a makeshift hair salon. She somehow had managed to get hold of a few hair products and had sat a dirty, old mirror on top of a shelf for her 'customers' to look in. She told me of her abusive childhood and how she had been caught up in the drug scene of Los Angeles. In order to pay her drug debts she had been talked into smuggling drugs out of Ecuador, but in the process had been caught at the border. She had been there for several years and did not know long how her imprisonment would be.

She had adapted well to prison life and seemed to command some respect from fellow prisoners due to her salon business. In the prison, there was a different kind of currency. After that first visit, I went back several times on my own, taking the bus and spending time with her. To help build some trust I asked if she wanted to cut my hair, which then was extremely long. When she had finished it was very apparent she definitely had not been to any school of hairdressing, just the school of hard knocks. I wrote to her after I left Quito, then one day was told that she had managed to escape from prison and I have no idea what happened to her after that.

The door is bolted behind me.
I begin to survey the scene.
Dark, unfriendly walls surround me:
I reflect on what might have been.
I had so much of this world.
Now I have nothing at all.
I used to think and act big.
Now my horizons are very small.
How quickly things change.
I just can't express how I feel.
Everything was so different,
now everything seems unreal.
Am I really here in prison?
What will become of me?
I have only just arrived,
but already I long to be free.
I used to enjoy such freedom,
if only to run and hide,
Now I am beginning to realise,
I didn't have freedom inside.
Deep within me, I was in bondage,
controlled by drugs and dope.
I thought I could do anything, but in truth,
I had limited scope.
I remember in my younger days,
when I was beginning life's search,
Of going down the country lane,
to the village church.
The words I heard there,
touched me in some way.
I kept them in mind,
for my future rainy day - AF.

Nana (far right) in the Molise traditional dress in Italy, circa 1940

Me outside Ashfield Valley Flats, 1972 in Dad's car (I have always loved being behind a wheel)

Nana (front) with one of her Italian friends, Puchi, in Rochdale

Dad and me, 1972

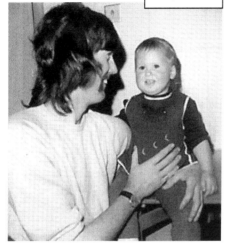

Me outside the Weaver's cottage on Mizzy Road (now demolished), 1976

My First Holy Communion. Photo taken on Cronkeyshaw Common, 1978

On our way out for the afternoon (Keri, me and Lou)

Me and Andrea doing a 'front angel' at SMG (on a chest of drawers on the second floor next to a single paned window!)

Grandad on one of the boat trips, Plymouth Sound, 1983

SMG Christmas Party - Far left: toasting with a mug of tea, Matron. From right to left: Miss Richardson, Lou, Me, Julia and Miss Scarlet, 1987

Skiing in Norway with Mum and David, 1987

David in the line-up for the Queen (in the foreground) Earl's Court, London, 1991

Michael's passing out parade, Harrogate: Nana, Michael, Me and Mum, 1987

Visit to Great-Grandma, Amy, with Uncle Kay at the Somerton House Hospice, Belfast, just before she passed away, 1991

Michael Mills (Mum's cousin in Ecuador) on a later trip to the UK, about to go up in a Cessna with Alistair

Patti and me working for Lehman Brothers in the World Financial Centre, New York 1993

Renee and me on the Observation deck at the top of the World Trade Centre (Twin Towers), 1993

Photo taken on the same day from the Observation deck

Children working in the fields with their mother with no shoes on their feet

Preparing our lunch, Guinea-pig soup, with cat looking on longingly

The intrepid explorers climbing Cotopaxi Volcano, the two English girls middle left (me second on the left, middle row)

Chapter Nine ∞ The Call Back Home

In September 1994, it was time to return to England to finish my Business Studies HND. Katrina, Sarah, and I along with a few others did a house share in another house on Blenheim Avenue. At the end of the course, I managed to gain a distinction which enabled me to transfer onto the final year of a business degree at Greenwich University. The business school of Greenwich was at Roehampton in South West London and I moved into Mont Clare Halls of residence at Minstead Gardens. I was very fortunate to have a room with an uninterrupted view of Richmond Park and would often see the deer nibbling on the grass in the morning.

At that time Roehampton was a running feature in the news. Two years earlier the murder of Rachel Nickell had taken place on Wimbledon common and police believed it was committed by a resident in one of the Alton Estate flats in Roehampton, a man called Colin Stagg. The Alton Estate is one of the largest social housing estates in the UK with its infamous five 11-story apartment blocks. Our halls of residence were in the shadows of these tall blocks of flats.

Police did not have enough evidence to convict Stagg. What followed was a catastrophic attempt to trick him into making a confession. He was convicted with little evidence and spent 13 months in prison. Stagg was formerly acquitted in September 1994 and as the true murderer was not convicted until 2008, there was still much suspicion surrounding the Roehampton resident. It felt like there was a killer on the loose in our neighbourhood. This was further highlighted when I was returning back to my room early one evening.

The halls consisted of several 2-story blocks in a cluster. As I was approaching my block I noticed that I was surrounded by police, some crouched down beside their cars, some lying down on the floor. Wondering if I had just accidentally stumbled into a live film set, all of sudden I heard one of them shout, "Quick, run, get into your room and lock your door". We had no idea what was happening but later found out there was a man prowling around our block wielding a machete.

I enjoyed my time in London and managed to gain a BA honours in Business Studies with a marketing major. For my dissertation, I supported the hypothesis that if a business is willing to engage in social responsibility and promote it through marketing strategies then it can actually result in increased profits. I used the co-operative bank as a case study.

During this year I started volunteering at a new radio station called Premier Radio, which had just launched on Chapter Street in London. It aims to enable people to put their faith at the heart of daily life. Each afternoon focused on a specific charitable organisation and it was my job to research them and write up a piece to be aired. I was offered one of the few paid jobs but it was not nearly enough to live on in London and I started to feel a strong pull to come back to Rochdale.

In the summer of 1995, I returned back home. By then Mum and David had bought and renovated a house on Lakebank in Littleborough with a great view of Hollingworth Lake, a 130-acre lake on the outskirts of Rochdale. During the early part of the 20th century, it became known as the 'weavers' seaport', due to its popularity with mill workers who holidayed there. It was originally built as the main water supply for the Rochdale Canal but developed as a tourist resort in the 1860s. This was helped with the arrival of the railway in 1839 when hotels started to be built. It subsequently declined and in the First World War, the area was used as an army camp. Since 1974 there has been a steady increase in facilities with restaurants, coffee shops, an amusement arcade, and a water sports centre. There is also a Rowing Club which has been in continuous operation since 1872. Captain Matthew Webb used Hollingworth Lake as a training camp before becoming the first person to swim the English Channel in 1875.

Alberto, the owner of an Italian restaurant on the lake front, then called the 'Del Lago', was kind enough to hire me, and again I worked behind the bar. It was an incredibly busy place on a Saturday night and inevitably it would be overbooked. I would spend the entire evening apologising for customers having to wait for a table and I often had to take the flack. It was three doors down from where we lived so there was no way of finding an excuse for being late and it was not far to get to bed after a busy shift.   Many years later we hosted my eldest son's christening party there for our family and friends.

When I came back I joined the Northern Employment Agency in search of a day job and was sent to various mundane office jobs.   It was a time when a lot of companies had only just become computerised and they all seemed to have a mile-high pile of information they wanted inputting into their new computer systems.   One day I was sent to the Rochdale Training and Enterprise Council on Sparrow Hill to fill a temporary role as a business librarian. They were based in an old grade 2 listed house that had been the former vicarage of St. Chad's Parish Church that was situated next door.

The church itself goes back to the year 1,100 and the town stocks in the grounds, used to put criminals in, is dated 1688. It had been built on land given by Adam de Spotland in an attempt to try and buy his way into God's good books. Ceadda, or later known as St. Chad, was born and educated in the 7th Century and mentored under St. Aidan in the monastery on Lindisfarne in Northumberland. He made several missionary journeys on foot in the north of England and it is believed that he founded the church in Rochdale. There is a window dedicated to him in the south aisle in which he is depicted preaching to Rochdalians.

The vicarage next door was originally built in 1724 for the Reverend Samuel Dunster who was a 'dignified clergyman and a useful magistrate' and was assigned to Rochdale in 1722. He adopted the plan for the vicarage from his house on Marlborough Street in London. It was now in the hands of Rochdale Borough Council and the home of Rochdale Chamber of Commerce and Rochdale TEC.

The library was filled with business journals, magazines, and books. Access to information on the internet was still very limited so lots of business people who wanted to research new markets overseas would often come in and use the books. After a few months in the post, the marketing manager gave her notice. Seeing that I had majored in marketing at university they asked if I wanted the job. I said yes and that was that.

Along with this role I was sent on an Export Documentation course along with another girl in the office called Caroline. Representatives from local manufacturing companies would come to us to get their export documents certified and stamped.

There was a great bunch of people working there and we had a lot of fun. Around this time the government launched a national business support network called Business Link. In many ways, it linked in with the business support offered by The Chamber of Commerce and so in Rochdale, there was a successful merger, along with the Rochdale TEC. I now had a marketing team of four to manage. We organised annual business award dinners, monthly networking events with key speakers, and a full training programme for small to medium-sized enterprises. We also wrote and issued daily press releases and developed a bi-monthly business magazine which we sent to every business in the borough.

As a government organisation there was often extra funding available for further training. I was sponsored to undertake an Advanced Post Graduate Professional Diploma in Public Relations which I completed at Leeds Metropolitan University in April 2000.

As with all government initiatives they go in cycles alternating between offering local outposts with centralisation, and in 2002 it was decided that Business Links were costing too much money and would become centralised. An email went out offering a voluntary redundancy package. By now I had my first boy, Ben and so had negotiated part-time hours, but I decided to take redundancy and re-join the family care home business. I very much wanted to be around Ben full time and I could take him to work with me at the Home.

In 1996 I had married Alistair. At that time I remember feeling quite desperate to settle down and have my own family. Whether it was because of all the moves I had made up to that point in my life or whether my biological clock was ticking I cannot quite fathom. By the time I was 21 I had lived in four different countries, four different regions of the UK, and around 21 different houses, including the various army quarters and SMG boarding houses. I don't think even gypsies move as much as that. I still now get itchy feet every few years and love the process of purging my belongings, packing up, and moving on.

Alistair and I met and married rather quickly, after only ten months of dating. On the 15th of June 1996, I had been shopping for wedding accessories in Manchester. That day the IRA decided to plant a 1,500-kilo lorry bomb, the largest bomb detonated in the UK since the Second

World War. It exploded at 11:17 am after 75,000 people had been evacuated; no one was killed because thankfully they had given sufficient warning. It caused the equivalent of £1.3 billion of damage creating a mushroom cloud that rose 1,000 feet into the air. The explosion was heard 15 miles away and it left a 15-metre wide crater. That event became the catalyst for the mass regeneration of Manchester, turning it into a modern 'powerhouse' city. A few years earlier my Uncle Damien Gabbott had a newsagent shop in Manchester's Arndale shopping centre. Strangely it was opposite Gabbott's Farm Butchers – which must be some distant relative as the name is so rare.

On the 10th of August 1996, I found myself walking down the aisle of Holy Trinity Parish Church in Littleborough in a handmade wedding dress. There was a man who lived in the village called Frank Kershaw who also attended the church. He made and still does make many theatrical costumes for shows around the country. The dress I wanted was far more money than I wanted to spend, or rather I wanted Mum to spend, so I took a photo of it for him and he made it for a fraction of the price. It was later donated to an African charity that seeks to enable vulnerable women to develop their entrepreneurial skills.

Mum and David were by now the sole owners of Meavy House Care Home, based on Milkstone Road in Rochdale. By the end of the first year, Linda and Griff had decided it was not for them and asked that they be bought out of the business. Meavy House was a lovely small family-run retirement home registered for 15 residents.

Nana had moved in after her stroke and several years later Grandad also moved in following his stroke. It was Mum's one consolation that she had been able to care so well for her own mother and father in the latter stage of their lives. It made up somewhat for not being able to move back to her beloved Plymouth. The house, Maker View, in Plymouth was reluctantly sold.

Just prior to his stroke, Grandad was already starting to make Meavy House his home. He loved the banter with the staff and generally enjoyed being around the buzz of the place. All his working life he had cycled to a sheet metalwork company in Royton, a distance of 14 miles. As he got older he would come to the Care Home and although he could no longer ride his bike, he would push it the four-mile round trip from Ennerdale Road and back. Whether this became a thing of habit or to act as a walking aid we will never know. During this time there was a national 'Come back to God campaign' which featured posters on billboards throughout the country. It seemed to be successful for Grandad as one day he announced that he had given his heart to Jesus.

I knew his conversion was real as a week later I was in a taxi with him and Nana. Just before he got out of the taxi to go back to his flat, he did something I had never seen before, he leaned over and kissed Nana on the cheek. Nana and I just stared at each other. Something had definitely happened with him. She looked quite taken aback but also had a wry smile on her face.

Across the road from Meavy House was a larger purpose-built Nursing Home registered for 32 residents, called The Lyndhurst. After some years it fell into financial difficulties and Rochdale council asked Mum and David if they would take it over. For ten years they ran both Homes side by side but over time costs began to increase. It became less economically viable to have the two and in 2005 they sold Meavy House to developers and wheeled the remaining few residents with their belongings over the road to the now renamed Meavy View Residential Home.

From the connections I had been made in marketing I was offered some hours as a public relations consultant with Catlow Communications, based in the Hardman's Business Centre in Rawtenstall. I also did some marketing work for a man called Dennis Freedman who had been blind since birth. Many years previously his wife had been in a car accident that had left her in a wheelchair. He made some cream, using a braille recipe, to help heal her skin. From that grew an organic soap, candle, and skincare business called 'Essentially Natural'. I still make my own moisturiser and candles now, inspired by Dennis. By 2003 my second son, George had been born and for a time I was a full-time mum, which I thoroughly loved. George was a textbook baby who would sit in his pram and watch the world go by.

Before long in 2006 a third boy, Jacob came along. Each of my three boys had been born almost three years and three months apart and my firstborn Ben had been born three years after we had got married. Three seems to be a prominent number. Mum decided that she wanted to ensure no one else was on the receiving end of the poor treatment she had endured when giving birth to me, so after her nurse training, she went on to become a midwife at Birch Hill Hospital.

I decided that I wanted her to deliver my babies. It was a wonderful experience and I felt really blessed that she had been the one to welcome them into the world. The Manchester Evening News caught on and we were covered in a newspaper article which headlined, 'Grandma scores a hat-trick!' She was always going above and beyond her duty as a midwife and would often help new mothers out with the various difficulties that can be experienced after giving birth. I nominated her for the North West Midwife of the Year Award which she won in 2006. We were invited to attend an Awards lunch at the Mamas and Papas headquarters in Huddersfield. She retired in 2013 after having delivered an estimated 3,000 babies.

Like all families of small children for a time life was a whirlwind of nappy changing, feeding, cleaning, washing, and keeping little boys occupied. I loved being a mother and for the first few years I home-educated them. We had a room in the house converted into a classroom with all kinds of educational, art and craft supplies. We enjoyed being creative and joining in with the regional home school network where we would meet up with others for learning and social days.

The look of innocence in a child
One minute calm; the next so wild,
Their ups and down of life we share
For through them all, they know we care,
They do things wrong; apologise
Then through their smiles and loving eyes
They win us over just once more
With dirty faces you can't ignore.
You can't be cross with them for long
As soon they fill the house with song.
In life they slowly make their way
Growing before you day by day
Their pleasures simple with joy they live
They find it easier to forgive.
They have their own sure paradise
A world of fun where people are nice
They are not crippled with earthly ties
They love the element of surprise.
So fresh and clean; their eyes so pure
their every movement firm and sure - AF.

Chapter Ten ∞ Flying High

"Lights, Camera, Action", Tim as producer, director, and actor sounded out the call. Another of Mum's cousins from America had got in touch to ask if her husband Tim could come and film a movie in Littleborough. It was from a script that he had written entitled 'The Commando'. It was to be a low-budget film so we offered to host him and the crew to save on expenses. The plot of the film was about a man who had served in the US marines in the Middle East. Whilst there, he had been in close proximity to an incendiary device that had exploded. This had left him with neurological issues. The film portrays his wife's struggles as she adapts to this new version of the man she had married.

Tim who plays Nick in the film gets a little helping hand from a local gym owner to start building himself back up again. He does so and then eventually takes on the town's bad guy and brings him down and becomes the hero. Tim had advertised the project and sourced actors and crew. The cameraman was flown in from Miami, another cousin, Matt, flew in from California to be a boom boy, and actors were recruited from Germany and England. The gym owner in the film was an actual gym owner called Sam Cullingworth from Osset, West Yorkshire and so we all drove over there to film the gym scenes.

To further cut down costs Tim recruited our family and friends to play certain parts. David was selected to be the bad guy and one of his lines was, "This is my town so get outta here!" something we still remind him of occasionally. In the film my UK cousin, Michael was in David's bad boy gang and I had a walk-on, one-line part. At one point in the film, the wife of Nick is considering putting him in a Care Home as she does not feel she can look after him. For these scenes, we used Meavy House and some of our residents were delighted to have parts to play in it.

It was a truly unforgettable experience and I admired Tim for pulling the whole thing off. We ended up hosting most of the crew and actors and there were tents pitched in our back garden and bodies sleeping all over the lounge floor. The script for the film did receive some awards, but the film was a little too low budget to go much further, though we do have the DVD to commemorate the event. I still sometimes say to friends, "See you later in the film" as life often feels like a surreal movie.

Alistair had always wanted to be a pilot. One day whilst looking for inspiration for his forthcoming birthday present I saw the perfect gift in an Argos catalogue, a voucher for a one-hour flying lesson in a light aircraft. When I handed him the gift, he said he knew he would not be able to stop at just one lesson. We all trooped down to Barton Aerodrome in Manchester and watched as he took his first flight. When he landed he enquired into the cost of doing his private pilot's licence (PPL). From memory, it was around £2,500, money we did not have.

After the lesson, his grandmother asked all about it. Alistair mentioned his desire to one day do his private pilot's licence (PPL) and there and then she offered to put half the money toward it. When his other grandma learned of this she did not want to be outdone and offered to pay the other half. At that time Alistair was working at the Yorkshire Building Society. He had secured a place on their graduate trainee scheme and had become the youngest share save account manager in the company. He had a good future ahead of him, yet flying seemed to be pulling on his heartstrings. Finally he took the plunge and gave in his notice and signed up for his PPL. (I found out later in the heart dissection lesson of my podiatry degree that heartstrings actually do exist and do provide part of the nerve centre).

Those looking to move on to do their commercial pilot's licence (CPL) after doing a PPL often become flying instructors. In this way, they gain the required flying hours to take their training to the next level. We would often spend our days down at the airfield. There is a café and small play area and the boys could watch the planes landing and taking off. However, like all things the novelty soon wore off. We would occasionally go up together. I have a photo of Ben when he was about five years old strapped into the back seat of a Cessna with the headphones on nonchalantly eating a packet of crisps as though he was taking a bus ride into town.

The current Barton Aerodrome, with its grass runway, was opened after the First World War to establish a municipal airport. It was opened as the sole airport for

Manchester on the 29th January 1930 with a large hangar and control tower which are now both Grade 2 listed buildings. In 1938 all services were transferred to the new Ringway airport, now Manchester's International Airport. At the outbreak of the Second World War, the Aerodrome was used as a base for RAF aircraft maintenance.

Each year the Aerodrome ran an annual Christmas party for the children associated with the club. The children would be invited and would watch Santa arrive by helicopter with a big bag full of presents for them all. Flying instructors are not very well paid as the bulk of the fee for a flying lesson goes on fuel and aircraft maintenance costs. I was a full-time mum and we did not have much money coming in. There was a time when did not have much food in the house and I decided it might be a good time to pray. Without saying a word to anyone, later that day David turned up with a black bin bag full of meat for the freezer.

By now Mum and David had moved to a bungalow with a third of an acre of land. It was perfect for active little boys and I was very grateful that they were only a short walk away. Their support in those years was tremendous. I am not quite sure how I would have managed without them as Alistair often worked long hours and was away often with overnight stopovers. His first job was with the regional arm of British Airways which has subsequently changed ownership many times. Sadly as his career progressed he spent less and less time at home.

Not having had children of his own, David took the boys under wing and now tried to instil in them that sense of adventure he had tried to instil in me. He was always accumulating cars, bikes, and ride-on mowers – basically anything with a motor, which would inevitably drive Mum to distraction. Frequently she would exclaim, and still does, "When are you going to sell all these things" as she would swing her arm over the driveway. Yet these things gave the boys endless fun. They once ended up with an old folk's mobility scooter which ended up being their favourite plaything to ride on around the garden. No doubt it had been left over from Meavy House.

But one motor David will not part with is his 1998 Volkswagen Transporter. It is his daily work van which is often fully loaded with rubbish for the tip or tools (which are removed at night along with the pies which he often buys from Smiths Bakeries in Castleton). The inside ceiling is hanging down complete with wires, and for the past 24 years has been in need of a full valet. For the best part of twenty years, it was a green colour and it seemed the whole town knew him for it. Whenever I would borrow it I would get numerous people beeping and waving at me thinking it was him. I don't think they were playing the waving game. The boys used to call it the 'love bus' when they were younger. When you would ask why, they would innocently exclaim, "Because Grandpa takes the old people out in it and so it carries love wherever it goes".

David must have acquired his love of motors from his own father, called George. George had been a mechanic at the former Jaguar garage on Manchester Road in Castleton. Due to his job, he always took care of all the cars in the family, something David has continued to do.

He frequently asks us what our tyre pressures are like and if we've checked our oil and water lately. George Fitton died suddenly of a heart attack in 1976 when he was just 47 years old. At the time David was in the Malayan Jungle with the army. It was a terrible blow and he was given compassionate leave to come home.

When on maternity leave with Ben I had started going back into the Care Home to help Mum out in the office. Ben was a terrible sleeper and seemed to need constant rocking. I would take calls and work on the computer with one foot rocking Ben in his car seat under the desk. Nana loved it when we came. She would have him in the pram and walk him in the rear courtyard garden. It was lovely to see her cooing over him as she walked round and round the water fountain. I know it brought her a lot of joy and for that I am thankful.

In 2010 I started the permanent job of book-keeper and office administrator for our Care Home which I did until the day it was sold in March 2017. Mum had been doing the admin and she wanted to return to full-time work at the hospital. My office was in the basement with a small window for light and air, but I did not mind. It felt a haven of peace compared to being at home with three young boys, though they were all by now at school.

Many of the staff had been working for us since we opened the Care Home, which by the end was 27 years, so we all felt like one big family. One who was very dear to us all was Anna Butterworth who had been working at the Home since the beginning. She was very petite and still looked in her twenties even though she was in her fifties

She wore a smile with every outfit and was one of those who had the ability to light up every room she entered. She never spoke a bad word about anyone and the staff and residents alike loved her. She was so full of love and warmth that whenever she was at work there was a tangible shift in the atmosphere. She had a deep concern for the residents and would often tell them all that Jesus loved them. When she died suddenly of heart failure one evening after work at the age of 60, it was a terrible shock for us all and she is still very sadly missed. There is a bench in the courtyard of Meavy View to commemorate her life and service to the Home. Sometimes the good ones leave us early.

As I write this story I am reminded that often life turns a full circle. In the early days of Meavy House, many of the staff were recruited from Zion church across the road. One such lady was Irene Manock, a lovely, kind, and warm person who was very good with the residents. Almost thirty years later we discovered that we lived on the next road from each other. Now being in her eighties, Irene has outlived all her immediate family with her only daughter, Andrea, having passed away with cancer at the age of 53. With me having no grandmothers left we have adopted each other and I consider her one of the closest people to my heart. She lives in a lovely cottage with the most beautiful little flower garden. People often stop and admire her garden and she is only too willing to share her heart of love with them, giving the little children who stop by little bouquets of flowers. She would have made a wonderful Grandma.

Another particular member of staff was Losana Kucuve from Fiji. She had come to England with her husband and had worked for the Fijian ambassador. She was a wonderful carer and very fit and active. She still works as many hours as they will give her even now in her late 60s and she often walks quite a distance before and after her shifts. She would sometimes spend Christmas with us and has always felt part of our extended family. Over the years Mum and David often invited people round. With David being a chef in the army; his cooking seemed to taste better the more people he had to cook for. They would often host barbecues and have people over for Sunday dinner.

We had another guest for Christmas one year, her name was May Price. May worked with Mum at the hospital and lived on her own. She brought her dog with her that day. It was the biggest black poodle I had ever seen, dispelling my belief that poodles were small things. When we were finished with dinner and were all relaxing in the lounge we started to wonder where the dog was. We went into the kitchen and the dog was on the floor with the whole turkey carcass in its mouth. Its head had been at the same level as the kitchen counter so he had decided what was left must have been his dinner. There were no turkey and cranberry sandwiches that year. May was very apologetic.

Over the years my marriage to Alistair had been experiencing significant difficulties. By now he was a Captain with Flybe Airlines and was away much of the time In January 2010 he was based out of Athens airport in

Greece and our marriage broke down completely. We tried to make it work for another two and half years but finally called in a day in 2012. Two years later Alistair remarried a wonderful woman called Charity from Nigeria. We have all remained on good terms, even going on holiday together to celebrate one of our sons 18th birthday.

Chapter Eleven ∞ Long Hot Summer Nights

Alistair could never get time off in the school holidays as the more senior pilots took priority and they all wanted them. So for the vast majority of the boys' childhood, I would take them on holiday with Mum and David. In 2001 they purchased an apartment in Nerja, on the Costa del Sol in Spain. We spent many a happy holiday there year after year and Nerja felt like a second home. Often friends and family would join us renting apartments on the same complex. As there were so many of us David managed to source an old, battered nine-seater Landrover, which we affectionately named White Betty.

He also got another toy with a motor one year, a jet ski, which of course the boys thought was brilliant - a motorbike for the sea. It could often be seen from the beach flying along the water with one of the boys behind David clinging on for dear life to the straps on his lifejacket. Of course, being boys they would demand he went as fast as he could, which David was only too happy to oblige. Sometimes it was better to shut my eyes.

Days were spent on the beach or by the pool, barbecues all together in the evening. Sometimes we would stroll down the Balcon de Europa. This viewing point sits on top of a cliff and separates the El Salon and Calahonda beaches. From there you can look out to sea or towards the Sierra Nevada Mountains.

Along the promenade to the viewing point would be various cartoon portrait artists, horses and carriages lined up ready to take people on tours, and the Green Man. My boys loved the Green Man – he was a street artist in a Robin Hood outfit but from head to toe was painted green. He would stand there like a statue unflinching and when he had enough of an audience would move and do all kinds of tricks. The boys enjoyed watching him so much they were even happy to part with their Euros to activate his movements. He also just happened to be next to the ice-cream 'helado' shop offering the biggest selection of ice-creams. The boys would be mesmerised by the different flavours and find it really difficult to choose, often just pointing at the nearest one.

On Sundays, we would go to Ayo's on Burriana beach for paella. Here at this beach restaurant, it seemed the whole of Nerja knew the secret - the best paella for miles around. It would be cooked out in the open in a large flat pan around six feet in diameter. The poor waiters would stand there with huge long-armed spoons stirring the pot. It was sometimes over 100 degrees and these waiters had to stand next to this blazing fire cooking up our dinner, we always left a good tip.

Another Chiringuito (or beach restaurant) which was a firm favourite was Pepe Oro's. There we would sit around a long table with sand between our toes and the boys would love to order baby octopus 'pulpo' and hake fingers 'meluza'. I preferred prawn pilpil, prawns served in a brown earthenware dish with olive oil, chilli, garlic, and flat-leaf parsley served with crusty bread and fried aubergines.

David had always been an avid fan of Thin Lizzy and he and Mum had seen them in concert in 1981 and 1983 at the Cornwall Coliseum in St. Austell. I was consequently raised on a steady stream of their music and I still seem to know most of their lyrics. Inevitably on the way back to the apartment after an evening stroll in Nerja, 'The best of Thin Lizzy' would be on the Landrover CD player. One song that we all loved was 'Dancing in the Moonlight'. We would sing it at the top of our voices as we drove the short journey back from Nerja along the N-340, a road that ran alongside the moonlit sea. The scenery around there is spectacular as the Sierra de Tejeda mountain range drops into the Mediterranean. The boys particularly loved the line 'I always get chocolate stains on my pants'. It seemed to resonate with them as often they had, from the ice cream they had just eaten. I still get a lump in my throat when I hear that song as I remember those 'long, hot summer nights'.

In the summer of 2016, Siobhan and Mark came from America and joined us whilst we were in Spain. Siobhan and I had always had a very close bond, the type where you could talk to each other about anything. That summer was known to be a particularly good one for watching meteor showers and it did not disappoint. As we laid out on sunbeds on the top terrace under the stars, we were treated to a spectacular light show. It seemed we saw shooting star after shooting star that night. It was so mesmerising and we lay there so long that we suddenly noticed the sky getting lighter and lighter. For a brief moment, we wondered what this strange phenomenon was until we realised that the sun was beginning to rise over the horizon. It was a deep and meaningful one that night.

One summer I was staying in a separate apartment on the same complex as everyone else with my two youngest boys. I woke up in the middle of the night and could not sleep. It was dark and I decided to go and lie on a lounger outside on the patio and look up at the stars. My bedroom was off from the lounge, so I walked through to the sliding patio doors which had a broken lock so remained ajar. I put the key in the lock of the metal gates just behind the patio doors and was about to turn it when I suddenly felt a strong compulsion to not go out. I decided instead to return to bed. I have learned over time to listen to this inner voice.

As soon as I laid down, I heard a loud rattling noise on the metal gates, I got up and went into the lounge and saw a man standing on a patio chair with a screwdriver in his hand levering his way into our apartment. You never quite know how you are going to react in these circumstances, I was glad I found there was a fight in me. My mind immediately went to my two young boys who were in the next bedroom. All I could think of was to make as much noise as possible, aware that I would wake the boys up, but also thinking it may be the only way to alert someone to the danger we were in.

I ran toward this man shouting out the most primeval scream I could muster until I was face to face with him. He continued to attempt to lever his way in through the metal patio grill, but just then a neighbour's light came on and he dropped down off the chair and ran. It is still a difficult thing to recall. The what-if questions set in; what if I had turned the key in the lock and gone out where he surely was? What if I had frozen and been unable to scream?

The next day my Spanish friend, Eddie, took me to the police station to give a statement and the police came to the apartment to look at the security. He showed me with what relative ease this man could have got into the apartment given a little extra time. It was a horrible ordeal and difficult to get through the rest of the three weeks of our stay there. I thanked God we were safe and well, but I did not take my eye off those boys for one second that whole trip.

In the summer of 2012, my marriage was totally over and my life was at a crossroads. I was now a single mum of three boys all under twelve years old and had no clue how I would manage. Whilst in Spain I started reading the ex-pat newspaper called 'Sur'. In there I read about an ex-pat couple who had retired to Spain. He was in a wheelchair and she had been his carer. The article proceeded to tell that the couple had been found dead, she of a heart attack and he had died later of starvation.

The story cut me to the core and started me on a train of thought. What could I retrain in which would enable me to help people in their own homes, provide a service that would add real benefit and something I could do anywhere in the world? I decided to open a Bible for inspiration Every page I opened mentioned something about feet

(Jesus washing the disciples' feet, Mary washing Jesus' feet, blessed at the feet of those who bring good news etc).

I decided to look up courses to do with feet and found that Salford University ran a part-time NHS-funded podiatry degree. To qualify for entry I needed to do a Level 3 Certificate in Anatomy, Physiology, and Pathology which I could do online through Oldham College.

As soon as I got home, I enrolled. The day I was writing the cheque for the course and signing my name on the dotted line. I started to get last-minute cold feet. Did I really want to do this? Would I be clever enough? I almost did not send it off, but with one last push, I decided to go for it.

I am so glad I did as it has been a very rewarding career path. This incident reminds me of the movie 'sliding doors'. The film alternates between two storylines, showing two paths the central character's life could take depending on whether or not she catches a train. Maybe it is not just in the major decisions in life but the minor ones that can totally affect our ultimate pathway.

Sometimes it takes just a little word
Perhaps when the battle is rife
To change the whole direction
Of a person's life.
A timely word in season
Perhaps from some unlikely source
Can steer a man's heart
On a much different course - AF.

I passed the online physiology course and in January 2013 took the train from Littleborough to Salford Crescent to begin my training as a student podiatrist. The University of Salford is one mile west of Manchester city centre. The former Royal Technical Institute of Salford opened in 1896 gaining university status in 1967. It has 21,500 students and is set in 160 acres of parkland on the banks of the River Irwell.

Around this time I had started going to a church in Manchester called Audacious. It was a far cry from the Latin Catholic mass of old and more like being in a nightclub. It was in a warehouse, with black curtains lining the walls, a full band, a smoke machine, special effects lighting, and an onsite café. There were about 5,000 people who would attend the various services on a Sunday, mostly students from the universities in Manchester. It was thriving. I discovered that they opened their doors to the homeless on a Thursday night. They would get a hearty meal, a free haircut, extra clothing, or the thing that was always in high demand – a dry sleeping bag. It was somewhere to come in from the cold, damp streets of Manchester. Yet what was desperately needed I was told, was someone to treat their feet.

The world seems more concerned,
with getting than giving.
Grab all you can it says,
Life is for the living.
Modern society with all its greed;
It's cunning and deceiving
Cannot conceive that happiness can lie,
More in giving than in receiving.
Offer what you can to others;
Loose yourself from the world's fetters.
Remember the happiest people are not,
the grabbers and the getters.
Let us truly be those people,
who with great joy believe
that it is always more blessed
to give than to receive - AF.

Chapter Twelve ∞ The Plight of the Homeless

"Hey how you guys doin?" was Sammy's usual greeting with a big smile from ear to ear and bear hugs to follow. The barber giving free haircuts on a Thursday night was Sammy Hernandez, a fun-loving bubbly guy from Puerto Rico who has been a good friend to us over the years. Another friend I met there was Vikki Turner. We instantly became close friends and had a lot in common which cemented our friendship. Since we met, we have been there for each other in good times and the bad, whether sitting with each other in A & E, ringing each other up in tears in difficult times, or simply being there as a sounding board for each other. Ironically everyone says we look like each other.

I helped organise Vikki's 50th birthday party at the Bellavista restaurant. Whilst her real sister was there on more than a number of occasions people thought it was Vikki and I that were sisters. Vikki surprised her husband that night by getting up from the table and taking over the drum kit with the band. She had been having secret drum lessons to surprise him. She is that kind of girl.

We have appeared on TV together twice. On one of these occasions we volunteered in helping transform a whole street in Manchester for ex-veterans which appeared on a show called DIY SOS. The second time was in a small audience listening to a talk by Boris Johnson before he became Prime Minister. He was on a campaign to convince us all that leaving Europe would be best for Britain 'Let's take Britain Back' was the slogan. Britain did finally exit the European Union on 31st December 2020.

My time at Salford University was a great experience. I loved being a student again and even loved getting the train in twice a week. I would stare out of the window at the dank, though strangely comforting, northern mill town scenery and reflect on life.

From day one we were put to work in the clinic treating real patients. The first few times were absolutely terrifying. We worried we would seem totally incompetent (on face value we were), and more worried we would cut off a toe by accident. We were taught to talk to the patients and make them feel at ease. One girl, who was hoping to be able to change her career and leave her job at Laura Ashley, was making small talk with a patient. Whilst cutting the patient's toenail, the nail shot off and landed at the back of her throat. She left the course not long after; I do not think it was for her. I have always kept my mouth shut when clipping toenails ever since.

We always had a tutor on hand to give advice and the patients, knowing it was a training clinic, knew what to expect. The cost for the treatment is also cheaper compared to private clinics so they did not seem to mind our initial ineptitude. The tutors assured us that being thrown into the deep end was the best way to learn. They were right and in no time at all, we felt like we had been doing it for years.

Having heard about the plight of the feet of Manchester's homeless. I knew in my heart that I wanted to be able to offer them a service and the need was immediate. After a few years of training at Salford, I discovered that the rest of the training was gearing us up to work in the NHS and covered topics such as biomechanics, surgery, and medicine. I knew that I wanted to offer a service to the homeless and the elderly in their own homes, so although the rest of the course would provide some background information it was a little surplus to my requirements.

It was then that I discovered the Alliance of Private Practitioners and found a college in Blackheath that took you through a one-day practical and theoretical assessment. If you passed the exam you were admitted onto their register and allowed to start practicing. I felt I had enough clinical experience under my belt and so I and another girl called Rebecca from Salford went down to try out for the exam. She too wanted to start her own private practice in Liverpool.

We were both really nervous and spent the previous evening in a local hotel with a glass of wine testing each other from the book 'Neale's Disorders of the Foot'. The next day we both sat the exam and to our delight, we both passed. We felt totally euphoric. To be able to start practising felt quite an achievement after so much hard work.

Around that time Salford University was offering social enterprise grants for students. I applied outlining my desire to start a foot-care service for the homeless. It was granted and I was given £500 which went some way toward purchasing all the supplies I would need. The NHS has also provided me with sterilised instruments for services to the homeless ever since.

And so I started a pop-up clinic on a Thursday night at Audacious church with Vikki by my side. At that time Vikki was a practice nurse in a GP surgery so provided an excellent advisory service to the men and women who would come through the doors. We also had a good system going. Sometimes there would be up to 20 people on the list. I would treat their feet, Vikki would take down their medical history, and then we would wash their feet and give them new socks and shoes. I was always truly humbled by the tremendous appreciation they would give. For many of them walking the rainy streets of Manchester day after day meant that feet would be sorely neglected and often very sore.

From a practice point of view, I felt my experience grew massively. I would have to treat such conditions as trench foot, nails that had never been cut and were now embedded in the sole of the foot, and terrible untreated ulcers. Things you would not usually see in private practice. Thankfully with Vikki there, we could offer a half-decent medical service.

On Saturday nights, Vikki and I had also signed up for street work. This involved making sure we arrived at Pret-a-Manger in Spinningfields, Manchester for the close of business at 9 pm. They would give us all their unsold fresh food, sometimes in bags so full, they would be difficult to carry.

Come rain, snow, or rare sunshine we would then trek the streets of Manchester in search of hungry mouths to feed. We would not have to walk far. There were the regulars in their fought-for spots, the most prestigious ones next to the cash machines and outside the corner shops up and down Deansgate. We would also go up toward Portland Street where we would often find new faces. Many of them we knew from the Thursday night sessions and if we did not recognise them, we would tell them where they could find us and get a hot meal.

Around this time a new guide had been produced outlining where all the services existed in Manchester for homeless people. We would give these out in waterproof covers with lanyards. It was always heart-breaking to see the younger ones new on the streets. It reminded us of our own boys, some of which were now of the same ages. We understood how easily family situations can break down and for many, there is no other option than to take to the streets.

After several years, and just one week before the 22nd May 2017 Manchester Arena bombing, our circumstances changed and we ended the service. Unlike the IRA explosion in 1996 for which warning had been given, this bomb killed 23 people. I visited the knee-deep sea of flowers in St. Anne's Square which demonstrated the outpouring of grief in the city.

During this time the Manchester Bee was resurrected to become a well-known emblem to remember those who had lost their lives. The Manchester worker bee has been an emblem for the city for over 150 years and is set in mosaic tiles in the town hall. In the 1800s Manchester was inundated with textile mills that were described as 'hives of activity' and the workers inside were compared to bees. Since the bombing, the bee emblem has appeared all over the city in huge murals to represent a resolute spirit to overcome terrorism and for a show of unity. These worker bees have been painted on the sidewall of the Koffee Pot café in the heart of the Northern Quarter, each bee to represent one of those who died in the attack.

I later found another place where I could offer a pop-up foot clinic to the vulnerable closer to home. I have had to learn over time that you cannot fix everybody all of the time, but I still feel compelled to do what I can, where I can. I was a single Mum and my priority would be to ensure my own boys had my support throughout their childhood years.

Now that I was certified I was able to launch out and offer my foot-care service to people wherever it was needed. An easy starting point was doing the feet of the residents in Meavy View and from there word got out and my business grew. The vast majority of my clients nowadays live on their own and I see how difficult life can be for them. Often I am the only person they see for days or even weeks. It is a privilege to go and see them and just make them feel better in some way, whether it is cutting their toenails, giving them a little foot massage, or telling them that Jesus loves them when they feel that no one else does.

Chapter Thirteen ∞ Strength in Hard Times

As I look back I see that in many respects I have had a very interesting life. We have not always had money, but the older you get you realise that whilst having money can alleviate the stress of making ends meet, it is the people in your life that make you rich. Of course, a memoir does not include all there is to recollect. There have been many tremendously difficult times along the way. Who has not had a share of pain and misery?

But the one thing that has got me through over the years is my faith. When I was 19 years old I had an experience that changed my life completely. Whilst I was working as a care assistant at Meavy House, I started asking the big questions in life. Why on earth are we here? What is it all about? It seems I am not the only one who has asked these same questions. On the internet, on keyworldtool it shows that among the recent top Googled searched terms are 'Who am I?' and 'Why am I here?'

In 1990 we were living in the flat above Meavy House. One Sunday the church across the road, the one we had bought the building from to convert into a care home, was having a special event. Mum said, "Why don't you go to the church over there and see what it's all about?"

It was a pivotal day that 7th October in 1990. There was a man speaking at the church called Jim Sweet, then in his 80s. He was telling the story of an incident that occurred when he was serving in the Parachute Regiment in the Second World War. One day having jumped out of the aircraft his parachute would not open. It had what was termed as a 'roman candle', where the jumper is entangled in the parachute making it look like a flaming fireball plummeting toward earth. As Jim was falling, he cried out to God to save him, as often people do in times of great danger. There and then he heard an audible voice telling him to pull out the two outer ropes. As he did, the shute opened and seconds later his feet safely touched the ground. It was from that moment that he dedicated his life to following the One whom he knew had saved him from certain death. Now he was here in Zion Church telling his story.

At the end of his message, he asked if there was anyone in the room who wanted to know Christ personally. A friend who was with me shot his hand up in the air and I tentatively followed by putting my hand up too. I had never known that faith can be on such an intimate and very personal level. Up to that point, Christ had always seemed to be just a figure in a painting or a statue. But at that moment, as the few that were gathered began to pray for us, I felt the sensation of a huge heavy burden being lifted off me. All of my life I had felt lost, but there and then in the deepest core of me, I felt found. I was then left with a euphoric feeling of joy which had me in tears for the next four hours. It was as though I had finally found what I had been looking for.

Around this time, my Auntie Ellie started to read her Bible and also had a spiritual awakening. Totally independently of each other, Mum also experienced the same. It was like something indistinguishable was sweeping through the family. It had started in the US with all seven of the cousins, Grandad's nieces and nephews, also coming to faith (one albeit later than the others) and it was this occurrence that brought a closeness between us all. From there Mum and I started going to Jim Sweet's house on a Wednesday evening on Ellis Fold in Norden, Rochdale and he helped us understand the Bible more clearly. Until then, the Bible just seemed like a boring old history book of some distant land. However, from that day on, it really seemed to come alive to me. Even now I frequently seem to be directed to read something in it and it will exactly relate to my situation and be what I need to hear.

I have seen over time that often our lives form a ripple. Much like when you throw a stone into still waters, the effect ripples outwards until it reaches the shore. When I was living in Slough doing my HND, Katrina, Kevin, Sarah and I decided to go to Slough Baptist church one day. Sarah had been raised in a Christian home so was no stranger to church. One day Kevin had a spiritual awakening and later decided to get baptised. At his baptism Katrina also had a similar experience and decided to become a Christian. Not long after that she went home and told her father about it and he had a similar experience. He ended up going on a trip to the Philippines and felt compelled to move there and help the people. He had been a builder by trade and has lived there ever since building a school, orphanage, houses, and a church for the desperately poor.

Still sometimes in life things happen when you know without a shadow of a doubt that your prayers have been answered. Lou and I lost contact a few years after boarding school. She went through a very difficult time and ended up deep in the Gothic scene. She had met a guy who lived in Manchester's notorious Hulme Crescent and decided to get away from significant difficulties at home and move up north to be with him. Hulme Crescent was then the largest public housing development in Europe, encompassing 3,284 flats and housing over 13,000 people. This was the 1980s and many were squatting and there were horrendous drug and gang issues. I did try to keep our friendship going and even went to stay with her in the flat they were squatting in. She took me around the gothic nightclubs in Manchester and introduced me to all her new friends.

I reminisced about the times we used to sit in our secret basement room and ponder what life was all about. Once I had become a Christian I felt like I had found some answers and wanted her to experience what had changed my life. Yet she did not want to hear at that time and we found we could no longer connect with each other and went our separate ways. Ten years later I found myself wondering what had happened to her and decided to try and find her. I wondered if she had gone back to her hometown in Dorset and I rang directory enquiries, there was no social media back then. I asked the telephonist if she could give me a number for a Louise Moogan in

Blandford Forum. She explained that she could not give out a number without an address, which I did not have, but in the next breath, she said, "Here it is …" and gave me the number. I rang it. Lou answered after just a couple of rings. She squealed with delight and was excited to tell me that she had become a Christian just a few weeks before and had been praying that God would help her get back in touch with me. We stayed in touch after that and she would often come and stay with us with her baby girl, Sammy. By then I was married to Alistair with my own growing brood of boys, so Lou and I would take them on day trips often to Heaton Park where they could all burn off energy.

Alistair's father and mother, Andrew and Alison Feakin also had their own story. They had met when they were both working for Bolton County Council and were married in 1965. When Andrew was 35 years old, he had an experience that he wrote about in the preface of one of his poetry books, 'In October 1978 for the first time in my life, I felt an overwhelming desire to go to church. Over time the words that the Vicar had to say in his sermons slowly began to mean something to me and the teachings of Jesus Christ began to mean more and more. In the summer of 1979, I could truly say that Jesus Christ had become a real living person to me; however, I was still very troubled. It was at a prayer meeting one evening that I asked that these hindrances be removed, that I could forgive and forget all the harmful things in my past. I wanted to feel like a new motorway just before it had opened, completely empty, the way ahead clear. The healing power of Christ began to work in me. He slowly and at times painfully broke down all the barriers to finally set me free.'

Andrew said of this time that a total transformation took place in him – a complete change of emphasis and direction with a feeling of internal peace, joy, and happiness he had never known before. From this time on he felt he was being directed to write poetry, something he had no experience of. By the end of the first month, he had written sixteen poems and he speaks of 'receiving them' not just 'writing them' with, on many occasions, the words simply flowing from his heart. Some of the first few he wrote is as follows:

I'm standing now before you,
A lone despairing lamb.
I know not what to say or do
Please take me as I am.
I look into your radiant face,
Your joy and peace so real.
Can You restore, rebuild, replace?
Before You now I kneel.
You look into my languid eyes,
You see my doubt and sin.
"I will forgive you all those lies,
And give you peace within."
Then Your caring outstretched hand
So firmly grips my arm.
"Don't be afraid just understand
My love, I mean no harm."
A gentle breeze now blowing,

Refreshes every part.
Your love now overflowing
A warmth just fills my heart.
My mind and body revive,
Your peace deep in my soul – AF.

Look for yourself, What do you find;
No lasting comfort, No peace of mind?
In the long run, disappointment, loneliness
Despair, rage, ruin, and decay
But if you look to Christ you will find all you need
So turn to Him this very day - AF.

By the end of Andrew's life, he had written over 6,000 poems, this equates to writing between 2 and 3 a week for over 40 years. He had an amazing way with words and would often write letters to prisoners bringing them messages of hope. Dr. Rafael Campo is a poet and a doctor and believes that poetry can bring actual healing to people. In a study at the University of Exeter, Neuroscientists discovered that poetry creates a 'pre-relaxation' state in our brains and that there is an increasing pleasure reaction to each verse heard. They found that poetry stimulates memory, facilitates introspection, and relaxes us. It also proved that there is something very special about the structure of the poetic text that generates pleasure. It seems that a poem a day could be good for our mental health.

Soon after Andrew had his spiritual experience Alison also became a Christian and they both moved to Littleborough. Alison was a wonderful keyboard player

She would lug her old, heavy, Casio keyboard around to old people's homes playing them some hymns and songs that the residents remembered and loved to sing.

During mine and Alistair's separation and subsequent divorce, they remained extremely supportive of me and we maintained a good relationship. For five years there was just a field separating our houses and I would often pop in with the boys whilst out walking our dog. They were always ready and willing to babysit whenever I needed them and Alison did so until she became too ill. They were the best set of in-laws I could have asked for.

On the 26th March 2015, Alison died of cancer at the age of 69. After being around a care home for most of my life with residents living up to their nineties and some into the hundreds, it felt a little too premature. Four years later on the 16th March 2019, Andrew also passed away with cancer aged 73; his funeral was remarkably held on the anniversary of Alison's death. They both knew where they were going. They had full assurance that this life is only the beginning. One of Andrew's poems seems to speak of his arrival on the other side.

Forward in life's journey,
Growing in You still more
My life stretched out before You,
Beyond the distant shore.
Securely in Your presence,
Directed by Your hand,
Rivers and oceans behind me,
Ahead clear golden sand.
I barely notice the pebbles,

Those little jarring knocks
As my stride is gently interrupted,
By stones and jagged rocks.
Mountains have become molehills,
Sweet song-birds fill the air
All the peoples of the earth,
Assemble before You there.
Then, just as they now offer themselves,
So in You, I humbly stand
Trusting in Your unfailing love,
My future firmly planned.
The days of searching are over,
No longer need I roam
Many miles I've travelled to reach the shores,
Now I'm going home - AF.

After the passing of Alison, Andrew had remarried a woman called Mary and they had been married for two years when he passed away. Not long before he died, he said to Mary, "I'm not sure why I wrote all those poems, no one's really all that interested in them anymore". Since then, I have been given the six lever arch files of Andrew's handwritten poems. He had produced around six printed poetry books, some of which can still be found on Amazon. It is my hope that I will be able to produce more. I was amazed at how inspiring they are and have been using them in blogs and to give out to my foot clients, who really appreciate them.

Mary is now one of my dearest friends and we have recently launched Mary Jo's Home Help as a means of reaching the many desperately lonely elderly people in our area who are finding life a struggle.

I was in the garage of the bungalow that Andrew and Alison had shared for 22 years when I spotted Alison's old Casio keyboard in the rafters. It truly is heavy, I think they must have built them with concrete blocks inside in those early days, but it gives out the most beautiful sound. I found a good YouTube channel (called simplified piano) that gives keyboard lessons and have been fulfilling a lifelong desire of learning to play. They both left me with two great gifts and I hope to carry on their legacies.

Andrew himself was from divorced parents and had a difficult relationship with his own father. Later in life they were able to reconcile and in memory of his father's death on 27th October 1980, he wrote this poem:

I can no longer pull the plough
I'm tired; it's over; take me now.
I come to You so unprepared
Somewhat timid, a little scared.
Just guide me gently by the hand
And lead me to Your wonderful land
Where peace and joy in abundance reign;
Oh Lord please take me home again.
Your strength and power engulf me now
As I take my final bow.
I thank You, You've granted my request
A home with You, a place to rest.
Now fast I'm drifting out of sight
Into Your world of eternal light - AF.

Chapter Fourteen ∞ Nana's Final Moments

Sitting by Nana's hospital bedside in 2008 we knew she would not last much longer. The previous evening she had been sitting up in a chair and I had been able to talk with her. Yet just twenty-four hours later I knew she was already gone, though she was still breathing. By January 2008 Nana had lived at our Care Home for 18 years but had developed heart problems and ended up at Fairfield hospital in Bury. Having been around the Home for almost three decades we had seen death many times and we knew all the signs of someone's last moments. Nana's breathing became much laboured and the colour washed out from her face.

We were holding her hand on either side of the bed and were both in silent prayer and contemplation. Just then as Nana was breathing out her last, there came a tremendous peace that entered the room, it was tangible. Mum said, "I can smell Him... Jesus". There seemed to be a phenomenally strong perfume scent that filled the room. What happened was quite indescribable, we loved her dearly, but the strange thing was that despite the fact that she had passed away, we felt only joy and not grief. We both had the absolute assurance that Nana had been taken and was now free from any pain and in absolute peace. As if for that moment heaven had come down to earth, and in heaven, it is said that God wipes away all our tears.

This reminds me of another time when I was with someone who was passing away. He was a resident in the Care Home by the name of Jack. Word got out that Jack was nearing the end of his life.

Sometimes relatives make it to be by their loved one's bedside in time; sometimes they are not able to and sometimes, for whatever reasons only known to them, they choose not to be. I was in the room alone with Jack when he entered the final stage of his life. His breathing became laboured and the colour washed out from his face.

I found the song 'Amazing Grace' on my phone and allowed the words to wash over him. Almost all elderly residents are familiar with the old hymns as once all children attended Sunday school. Before long Jack was breathing his last few breaths. Just as he gave one last gasp, a shaft of light shot through his bedroom curtain. That day Rochdale's usual grey clouds parted to light up Jack's face before he departed from this world. Who knows what takes place between a soul and God in those final moments, if one gets the chance?

Out of darkness into light,
Into a world that's shining bright.
Out of gloom and total despair,
Into a world of loving care.
Out of disaster and deep distress,
Into joy and happiness.
Out of a life of misery,
Into a world that's full and free.
Out of the day and into night,
There is no darkness in Your light - AF.

Several years ago, I was asked to go and visit a new client in Hare Hill, an assisted living house in Littleborough. I walked into his flat and noticed a crucifix on the wall. As we got talking and I started to do his feet, I found out he had been a teacher. I asked which school, "St. Patrick's in Rochdale", he replied. We soon put two and two together and realised he had been my upper primary school teacher.

It had been almost 45 years and I could not believe he still remembered me – "Ah yes Joanne Gabbott", he said. He also remembered my friend Sara Twigger and her mother. She had since passed away with cancer but was very much remembered in St. Patrick's parish for making the banners in the church.

There are some clients who you thoroughly enjoy visiting and Mr. Simkins was one of them. We would talk about school days and about faith. He had a great sense of humour. One day I went to do his feet and he was not there. I later found out that he had fallen and had been taken to hospital. He had since been moved to a Care Home and his family asked if I would go and see him and continue to do his feet. They could not go and see him due to the restrictions that were in place and so they asked if I would spend extra time with him.

He had become very frail and after doing his feet I asked if he wanted me to read to him. He responded with an enthusiastic "Yes". So I pulled up a blog post for that very day which was from Psalm 39. And I read, "This Psalm teaches us the brevity, uncertainty, and calamitous state of human life. King David asks God to make him aware of the shortness and uncertainty of life and the near approach of death that will come to each of us. 'Lord, make us to consider this, that we may secure our mansions in heaven, not made with human hands. It declares that our anxieties are often groundless and we disturb ourselves in vain, for we cannot, with all our anxieties alter the nature of things. Things will be as they are, even when we have vexed ourselves over them. But King David soon turns his eyes and heart heavenward. Now he began, more than ever, to look upon himself as a stranger and sojourner here. He was not at home in this world, but travelling through it to another, and a better one, and would never reckon himself at home till he came to heaven."

As I was reading, I suddenly remembered reading to Mr. Simkins at his desk from the Peter and Jane reading books over 40 years ago, as a small girl at primary school. I marvelled that here I was again reading to him, now in a Care Home in the closing days of his life. All I could do was silently thank God for His amazing and mysterious ways. Life often does come full circle.

I looked at Mr. Simkins and asked if he wanted me to pray for him. He again responded with a "Yes". We both had tears in our eyes and he was reluctant to let go of the grip he had on my hands. He kept thanking me over and over, asking God to bless me. He passed away not long after. There are few moments in life that are more precious than the likes of those.

My life was so empty, lost, and forlorn.
At times I wished I'd not been born.
For me no hope or future in life,
Just constant battles of meaningless strife.
Where is the purpose here for me?
Will someone help that I may see?
Then slowly things began to change;
At first it seemed a little strange,
A different feeling deep inside,
A peace and joy you cannot hide,
A whole new world so fresh and new,
A deepening love so strong, so true,
A whole new power in Jesus' name.
My life will never be the same! – AF.

Chapter Fifteen ∞ And as the Queen Said

In 2011, Queen Elizabeth II was quoted as saying, "Although we are capable of great acts of kindness, history teaches us that we sometimes need saving from ourselves – from our recklessness or our greed. God sent into the world a unique person – neither a philosopher nor a general (important though they are) – but a Saviour, with the power to forgive."

No one with all their wealth and power has ever impacted the world as powerfully as Jesus Christ. Although He spent only three years ministering up to the time of His death and He travelled no more than two hundred miles from where He was born, yet more than 2,000 years later He is the linchpin of the human race. As a nation we celebrate His birth at Christmas and His death at Easter, we often choose to get married or have a baptism in a church and many would put 'Christian' in a tick box on a form.

But in our nation, the knowledge and understanding of who Jesus was, and is, is being rapidly lost. In 2018, I got the chance to go to Israel with three friends, one of whom was Den Smith. He had been to Israel before and acted as our personal tour guide. We spent the first few nights in Jaffa, near Tel Aviv then moved on to Galilee and finally spent a week in Jerusalem. We drove around visiting the key places where events in the Bible took place. I have been to quite a few places in the world but this has to be, without doubt, the most fascinating place on earth. It has taken centre stage in world events throughout time and is steeped in history. On-going archaeological digs are constantly affirming that the facts in the Bible are a hundred per cent accurate. It is here that the Bible truly comes alive. The scenery around Lake Galilee in particular is exactly as it would have been in Jesus' day. The atmosphere there is sublime, almost as if there is a portal to heaven in that very place. Just maybe there is.

> Heaven on earth; our longing eyes see
> In the beauty and majesty of Galilee.
> As we look to You, who we adore
> We remember how, You walked this shore.
> As our eyes move, from hill to hill
> Somehow it seems, the years stand still.
> Our senses revive; we become more aware
> Of Your great love, we long to share.
> We touch the shore; we hold Your hand
> As together in love, we walk the land.
> A boat, a fisherman, oh how sublime
> Caught up in eternity, but living in time - AF.

It is an incontestable fact that Jesus was born more than 2,000 years ago in a town called Bethlehem in Judea (now called Israel). There is a film called 'The Case for Christ' which is based on a true story. The film follows a journalist for the Chicago Tribune, who is an atheist and seeking out facts to disprove his wife's Christian faith. With his investigative reporter experience, he gathers information and evidence but concedes in the end that Christianity must be true.

On 21st December 2020, Jupiter and Saturn came together in a 'great conjunction' unlike any seen for nearly 800 years. The two planets appeared so close together on that winter solstice night that they looked like a single object. Some referred to this as the 'Christmas Star,' and wondered about similar celestial events that coincided with the biblical first Christmas and the Star of Bethlehem.

The story of the Star of Bethlehem appears in the Book of Matthew. It tells us that a bright star appeared in the eastern sky when Jesus was born, famously seen by a group of wise men. To them, the new star was a sign of the birth of the anticipated new King and Saviour of the people, so they set out for Jerusalem to worship Him. 'The star, which they saw in the east, went before them, till it came and stood over where the young child was and they rejoiced with exceeding great joy.'

There are more than 300 prophecies in ancient manuscripts concerning the details of the birth, life, death, and resurrection of Jesus – all of which accurately took place. Dr. A. Pierson stated that according to the law of probabilities, the chance that they could all happen together by accident is 1 in 537 million.

Jesus was raised in Nazareth. When the time came, He moved to Galilee where He began His work of proclaiming the Kingdom of God to whosoever would listen. For three years He went around the region healing the sick, driving out demons, raising the dead, and teaching the people. He challenged the hypocrisy that He saw in the religious leaders of that day, as I believe His message still does today. So they retaliated and sought ways to trick

Him and have Him arrested and ultimately killed. Little did they know that even in so doing they were fulfilling prophecy.

In Isaiah 53, again written almost 750 years prior to Christ's birth, it says that He would be despised and rejected; that He would be wounded for our wrongdoings, and that by His stripes (the Roman whippings) we would be healed. It went on to foretell that His grave would be made among the wicked (He hung on a cross with a thief on each side); and that He would bear the sins of many. It was all part of the Father's great plan to restore humankind to Himself and make atonement for the wrongs and guilt in us all.

A famous text that we have all probably heard is, 'for God so loved the world that He gave His one and only Son, that whoever believes in Him shall not perish but have eternal life'. Another common Googled search term is, 'What is love?' This is real love. All other love is fleeting. This love, unlike Mills and Boon's love, is unswerving and unfaltering. I can testify that God's love has never failed me. Life may not have turned out as I thought it would, yet His love has been there to lift me up. Lift me up above waves of depression, bring me peace in the chaos and hope when it has felt like all hope is lost.

One of my sons recently asked me what the difference is between Christianity and the other faiths. replied with, "In other faiths, you have to do something to earn your way to heaven, but God knew in our fallen, weak state we could never hope to reach Him, so He reached down and rescued us instead. He sent His Son to pay the price that was far too big for us to pay and so give us the assurance that we can be certain of everlasting life". For as it is written, "Everyone who calls on the name of the Lord will be saved". When this happens it is like finding a pearl of the greatest treasure.

> The happy merchant,
> His mind in a whirl,
> Goes and sells everything he has
> To buy that pearl.
> But even the pearl
> Will one day,
> Like all earthly treasures,
> Fade away.
> The pearl of great value,
> Have you found it my friend?
> Do you joy in that new beginning
> that can know no end? – AF.

According to The International Bulletin for Missionary Research (IBMR), there were over 559 million Christians around the world in 2015 and by 2050 trends show it will exceed any other belief. According to the Guinness Book of Records, the Bible is the all-time best-selling book consistently outstripping all other books with around 5 billion copies currently in distribution.

Following Jesus' teachings is not for the faint-hearted. Yet we are promised a life of fruitful abundance and life everlasting. This world and its pressures and pleasures will all too soon pass away. The day is fast approaching when all our earthly treasures will count for nothing. Our reputation among others will count for nothing.

It says in the book of Matthew, "But what profit is it to a man if he gains the whole world, but loses his own soul?" There is a line in a song called 'Wake me up' by Avicii that goes, 'I didn't know I was lost, I didn't know I was lost, I didn't know I was lost'. I believe this speaks for many of us, though if we are truly honest most of us have a sense that there must be more to this life.

Jesus stands at the door and knocks. He is knocking at the door of our hearts and asking to be let in. To be let in to walk this walk of life with us and help guide us in the small decisions and the big. Will we open up and let Him in? In the last book of the Bible, Jesus is saying "Behold, I stand at the door and knock. If anyone hears My voice and opens the door, I will come into him and dine with him, and he with Me".

> The Giver of all things
> He does understand
> Take a look at yourself
> Where do you stand?
> The choice is yours
> You can stay as you
> Or you can draw close to Him
> From your position afar - AF.

As Jesus was leaving this earth, His friends were sorrowful He said, "It is good that I am going away. Unless I go away the Advocate (or helper) cannot come to you. But if I go, will send Him to you". I have come to understand that rather than being a little, red flickering flame in a glass jar behind an altar – the Holy Spirit is much, much more than that. He is God's Spirit and our Helper and Comforter who promises to be with us if we invite Him in.

I have also come to realise that I can believe what the Bible says. When God says in His Word, 'Trust Me' I know through experience that I can. There have been many instances when I have seen His hand at work in my life. Like the day our cupboards were running low and a freezer load of food arrived on my doorstep or like the day my car repair bill came to $103.15, exactly to the penny I had to my name. I also believe we were protected that time in Spain when I came face to face with an intruder. Looking back over my life I can also see how many near misses I have had when the outcome could have been very different had time or space been slightly adjusted.

Though I have had to go through some incredibly difficult and traumatic times, not all of which have been recorded here, God has met my every need and proved beyond a shadow of a doubt that He is faithful and that He is true.

Who can be trusted,
when the battle is rife?
Is there anyone you can trust,
with your life?
Who can you depend on,
when the going gets tough?
Who is it who will make smooth,
every path that is rough?
Who is it who can go ahead,
to prepare pathways new?
Who can take away all falseness,
to bring all that is true?
In the heat of the battle,
amidst the rising dust
Is there one in whom,
you can put your trust?
In all the uncertainties of life,
there is one thing you can do
You can place your trust,
in the Man who died for you - AF.

Chapter Sixteen ∞ Walking in Saint Chad's Steps

I took the long scythe and began hacking away at the brambles and nettles that had overgrown along the coastal path. It felt as though there was more than a physical action taking place, something much deeper. Along the Essex coast is an off-grid community called Othona near Bradwell-on-Sea.

The first morning I arrived at Othona I had risen early to watch the sunrise on the beach, a favourite pastime of mine when by the coast. As I made my approach, I found that brambles and nettles had overtaken the path. Determinedly I pushed my way through. As I did, I had a sense that this was a picture of my life. We all have a path before us and a race to run, yet often we are hindered from running by things that hold us back, things often only known to ourselves.

Sweating in the summer sun, scythe in hand, the task seemed a little daunting. Yet I was resolute. The path also links Othona with an old Observation Tower which had been part of the nearby World War Two RAF Bradwell Bay Airfield. The tower, now in disrepair, forms a very stunning and dramatic backdrop for landscape photography and paintings. Sometimes we are in need of standing on such an observation tower to reflect over our lives. What are the things in our way preventing us from running our race?

I will climb my watch-tower now,
And there in peaceful restraint
Wait to see what answer,
I will get to my complaint.
The time is coming quickly
What I show you will come true
It may seem slow in coming
But patience I give to you.
Build a tower of expectation
Believe there is an appointed hour
When all that is beautifully anticipated
Will be manifested in great power – AF.

There is something about community living that appeals to me. Maybe it is seeing all those desperately lonely, old people that I do the feet of, maybe it is seeing the decline in community spirit over the years, or possibly because it is familiar to me from boarding school. I realise it is not for everyone and I am not quite sure that it is actually for me. Yet I think there is something to be said for living together, eating together, and sharing life together. If there were more of it maybe there would be far less of a pandemic of loneliness and addictions that plague our nations.

In 2001, Portugal decriminalised the possession and consumption of all illicit drugs. The money that had been used to haul drug offenders through the legal system was instead pumped into funding community projects and work schemes for them. The results have been staggering. The country has seen a dramatic drop in overdoses, HIV infection, and drug-related crime. It seems that building community and giving people hope and a purpose is the answer to many of our problems.

Den Smith, my tour guide in Israel and personal friend, is in the process of building a community in Tomar in Portugal. I love Portugal and have been over quite a few times to help with the renovations. It is like the land where time stands still. It is the oldest country in Europe with unchanged borders since 1297, but more importantly, it has brought Peri-peri chicken to the world! In Tomar, as in other towns throughout Portugal, many locals head to the 'Churrasqueria' – the grill-house where you feed exclusively on chicken choosing simply how much you want to eat and how spicy you want it. It usually comes with fries and a side salad and an extra bottle of Piri-piri oil. In Portugal it is known as Frango Assado com Piri-piri. Piri-piri is a sauce made from lemon, salt, oil, and chili.

Each lunch and dinner time, if you are within a few hundred feet of one of these grill-houses, you can smell it and see billows of smoke blowing from some vent or other. You know it is time to eat from the queue of people all lining the street to either eat in or take away. On entry, you will find the cooks flipping around fifty spatchcock chickens at a time on a huge grill whilst routinely pasting them in Piri-piri sauce. When we are there we frequent them often.

The Portuguese were world-renowned explorers and are known to have spread chilies around the world. In 1498 Mozambique became a Portuguese colony and the chili first linked with Piri-piri was found here. It is believed that this chili was taken back to Portugal and from there a recipe formed which spread to the rest of the world.

It was in Portugal where I learned to mix cement and would carry it to Den who was often high up on scaffolding rendering one of the many walls. He has purchased buildings and land overlooking a 500-year-old aqueduct that once carried water from the purest streams to the 900-year-old Convento de Cristo in the centre of Tomar, which is now a world UNESCO Heritage site. One of these streams runs directly under the property and there is a well at the bottom of the land that never runs dry.

The land happens to be along one of the routes of the Camino de Santiago known in English as 'the Way of St. James'. This network of pilgrimage routes leads to where legend has the burial site of the Apostle St. James, in the cathedral of Santiago de Compostela in north-western Spain. In 1942 it was officially declared to be one of the 'three great pilgrimages of Christendom'. The main pilgrimage route to Santiago follows the Atlantic coast of Northern Spain (Galicia) and ends at Cape Finisterre on the Western edge. At night, even the Milky Way overhead seems to point the way, so the route acquired the nickname 'Voie lactée' – the Milky Way in French.

The scallop shell often found on the shores in Galicia has become the symbol of the Camino de Santiago which is placed on markers throughout the various routes. There is one at the top of the road where Den lives. Each year hundreds of thousands of people leave their homes to make their way along one of the routes, usually on foot sometimes by bicycle, and some even on horseback o donkey. There are guides printed each year with places where pilgrims can eat and sleep along the way, often at the kind hospitality of the locals.

Most pilgrims carry a document called the 'credencial' or 'pilgrim's passport' which is stamped in each town or refuge where the pilgrim has stayed. The 'Camino Portugués', or the 'Portuguese Way' consists of 610 km and is the second-most-popular route which starts at the cathedral in Lisbon crossing into Galicia at Valença. In the film 'The Way', the leading actor, Martin Sheen, learns that his son had died along the northern route and he takes up the pilgrimage to complete it on his behalf. Many complete the pilgrimage as a form of retreat for their own spiritual growth and enjoy the new community that is found in the journey. It is another one on my bucket list.

Wherever I have been in the world, a good local church has provided a sense of community and instant family for me. Of course, sometimes I have had to visit a few different ones before I have found one that feels like home. Maybe this is why there is so much diversity in church styles, for we are a diverse people. I remember in that remote spot in Ecuador after our guinea-pig soup we decided to gather together with the villagers. Pablo took out his guitar and started playing some tunes and everyone began to sing in their native language. They were familiar tunes from songs sung in other places I had been. I marvelled that although my life and culture were worlds apart from these people, and despite our language barrier, at that moment we were as one. We smiled at each other with a common deeply spiritual 'knowing'.

In search of what community means my youngest and I found ourselves staying in an Indian yurt with a log burner within the grounds of Othona in Bradwell-on-sea. The Othona community had been founded in 1946 by Norman Motley, who served as a young chaplain in the RAF during the Second World War. He and his friends had found a comradeship in wartime that lowered many social and religious barriers. After the war, they wanted to preserve something of that and began to gather as a community each summer.

It started with just a few families, now there is a worldwide community of people who have visited, with many returning year after year. Many who go to Othona are of no faith, some do have faith but some go simply because they have been going all their lives and they feel the magnetic pull of the place. It attracts people from all walks of life, the rich, the poor, the old, the young. Yet there all are equal and you instantly feel part of something bigger than yourself. When there, we all eat together, and twice a day we all walk over a wheat field to one of the oldest and simplest chapels in England, dating back to 654 AD called St. Peter's-on-the-wall.

In Roman times the area was a defensive fort called Othona. After the fall of the Roman Empire, the fort became a village that St. Cedd or St. Chad arrived at in 653 AD. Chad built the chapel and dedicated it to St. Peter using the stones and tiles from the old Roman fort. Whilst there I discovered that the same St. Chad that had founded St. Chad's church in Rochdale was also the one to have founded St. Peter's-on-the-wall at Bradwell-on-Sea in Essex

220 miles away. Unbeknown to me I had followed in his footsteps.

The chapel itself attracts over 1,000 pilgrims a month travelling through Essex along the St. Peter's Way. One thing that struck me whilst I was there is that we are all sojourners in this life. We are all on a journey of discovery whilst residing in this temporary place called Earth. The chapel at St. Peter's-on-the-wall provides a unique place to be able to spend a short time of reflection. It is a tranquil and breathtakingly beautiful place. A place where you can go to get your soul restored.

> Never allow your heart to stray,
> By looking to the left or right
> You are on a beautiful journey, a pilgrimage,
> The end is not yet in sight - AF.

Othona sits in a remote area on the coast of the Blackwater Estuary, so it is only possible and safe to swim at certain times of the day. At low tide, a bell will ring and whoever desires to, walks down to the beach to immerse themselves in the cold, tidal waters. I am told it is good for the immune system. I did it for the sake of my son who coaxed me in and called me a chicken if I didn't. One thing that I love about the beach at Bradwell is the abundance of shells, in particular oyster shells.

The Blackwater Wild Oysters grow on the river bed of the Blackwater Estuary and begin life as a spat drifting about on the tide until it finds a stone or shell to attach itself to. Here it will settle indefinitely, into a routine of heavy drinking. It filters up to 10 litres of water per hour and feasts on the nutritious waters of the tidal marshlands. This fact reminds me of how I was drifting until I found that rock of faith at the age of 19 and began to drink of its waters and allow it to feed my soul.

At Othona in 2021 it was another notable year for shooting stars. There were a few times when we would all go to the beach for an evening fire, toast marshmallows, and a singsong. After chapel that night we spotted a man alone in the middle of the field with a remarkable assortment of cameras set up ready to capture that night's display. It turns out that Bradwell-on-Sea with its lack of light pollution is the perfect location to view the stars. When I look up at the clear, night sky I marvel at how incredible this world truly is. A world so intricately woven together that it must have been made by design. If by design then it must have a Designer.

The singing birds high in the trees,
The leaves that whistle in the breeze,
The driving rain, the howling gales,
The warm fireside, the wintry tales.
The lambs that frolic in the field,
The sunlit walk across the weald.
The roaring thunder passing by,
A rainbow glistening in the sky,
The snow that softly falls around,
The noise when hailstones hit the ground.
The new-born baby's wakening cry,
The treasured smile, the twinkling eye.
A friendly wave across the street,
The joyous look when first we meet,
A child's laughter fills the air,
A loving mother's tender care,
So many things for me to please,
I see you Father in all of these - AF.

It has been suggested that there are as many angels as there are stars and that each angel and fallen angel are closely linked with a particular star. The term 'heavenly host' in the Bible is used interchangeably in reference to both angels and stars. In the book of Job (pronounced Joab) God is challenging a man and essentially saying, "How can you know anything? Where were you when I laid the foundations of the earth? Where you there when the morning stars sang together and all the sons of God shouted for joy?"

The jury is still out regarding what we actually see when we look upwards. Many purport theories as though they are fact, when in fact they are not.

Robert Jastrow (1925 – 2008) an Astronomer, Planetary Physicist, and NASA Scientist said, "Astronomers now find they have painted themselves into a corner because they have proven, by their own methods, that the world began abruptly in an act of creation to which you can trace the seed of every star, every planet and every living thing in this cosmos and on the earth. And they have found that all this happened as a product of forces they cannot hope to discover. That there are what I or anyone would call supernatural forces at work is now, I think, a scientifically proven fact."

The famous Theoretical Physicist, Albert Einstein who lived from 1879 to 1955 was quoted as saying, "The more study science, the more I believe in God". Rather than disprove God, he and many other scientists are discovering that science proves there is a God who created this world that we find ourselves in.

Epilogue ∞ And so I did

Body recharged; a stifled yawn
Echoes its welcome to the dawn
Song-birds offer their sweet refrain
As sunshine glistens on a windowpane.
Those who weary of sorrow and sinning
I offer you a new beginning
For morning awakes to a freshening dew
To those who have died; all things become new.
Every day is filled with hope
Glorious opportunity and limitless scope
For I bring an end to misery and pain
Take the joy of a new day and begin again - AF.

I have spent a lot of time daydreaming about how to plan an escape from Rochdale. For several years I did manage it, but somehow could not resist the invisible force that pulled me back. Having now delved into the history of my home town I have realised the important role it has played on the world stage and I now have a new appreciation of the place where I was born and still live. I am even beginning to see more of its beauty and enjoy its familiarity and focus less on its undesirable aspects. I realise that it is not so much about the hand we are dealt with, or the situation we are placed in, but the lens through which we view it.

As I was staring at the candles on my 50th birthday cake I realised that I feel more sublimely content than I ever have done before. Not that there is an absence of difficulties for there are still a few of those, but the inner contentment in my own skin and a deep peace within my soul. It has been incredibly cathartic to write down all my memories to form this book. Sometimes it is hard to see the overall picture of our lives as we tend to focus on the here and now or tentatively look toward the next step. Yet to write your experiences down enables you to see how all the small moments add up to a more complete picture.

I could look back at SMG and feel resentment for the best part of my teenage years that were spent there, and for a few years, I have to admit that I did. Yet now I am grateful for the discipline and independence that was instilled in me during my time there. Nowadays SMG would never pass a CQC inspection and pupils would be posting photos of the conditions on social media and ringing child-line to have the place closed down. Whilst I am not advocating that mistreatment should be tolerated, it does bother me that today we do all we can to ensure our children are shielded from all and every difficulty. I wonder sometimes if this will not render them less capable of coping with life when real troubles come.

The more you mature in years, the more you realise that it is in the more challenging times of our lives that we have the opportunity to blossom as individuals. For in them we have the opportunity for our character to be strengthened and our empathy deepened for others, who also go through similar difficulties. Like the priceless oyster pearl that is fashioned as a natural defence against an irritant or damage done to its body. Like the stars that shine all the more brightly the darker the sky.

John Bright was spurred on by the grief caused by the loss of his wife and child, causing him to turn those moments of pain and anguish into the drive to reform laws for the good of the poor. John Ashworth, following the death of his wife, went on a search for purpose and became increasingly concerned for the poor resulting in establishing schools and churches for them. He spent his money on some of the poorest and saddest cases and helped many broken men get back on their feet. My own mum's harrowing childbirth experience led her to become a midwife to ensure others in labour had a much better time of it. We also ought to reflect with genuine gratitude for all the struggles throughout the years, for they often serve to redirect us and make us who we are.

Someone else who was born at a time of profound struggles was King Wenceslas. It was a time of great political unrest with deep power struggles between good and evil. Instead of being a victim of these struggles, he sought to carry the Christian message into a troubled world. We ourselves can often be the sufferers of trouble and violence of varying sorts and can easily identify with his difficulties and of his desire to experience peace and harmony in this world. Wenceslas responded to the call by being involved in action for social change. We, in our small circle of influence, can decide to do all the good we can do, and forgive those who have harmed or offended us, even when we do not feel they have deserved it.

The cross is the fundamental symbol of Christianity, some wear it on a chain, and some may have it on their wall. It is here where our lives were bought back. It was here where Christ died a death in our place, an act that we have not deserved. He paid the price of a cruel death and it is here that I look when I struggle to forgive others. Here I am humbled, and realise that I also am in need of forgiveness, for when I look in the mirror of my soul more closely, I sometimes see the same imperfections in myself that I am quick to bring the accusation of in others.

During King Wenceslas' journey, his aide was about to give up but was enabled to continue by following the king's footprints, step for step, through the deep snow. The message here is that in following in the footsteps of those who have gone before us, we also can be guided on in our journey. Jesus said, "Come, follow Me", I am fairly sure King Wenceslas was following in the footsteps of the man, who less than a thousand years before he had been born, had come and changed history forever. The final verse of 'Good King Wenceslas', the carol reads:

'In his master's steps he trod, where the snow lay dinted, heat was in the very sod, which the Saint had printed Therefore, Christian men, be sure, wealth or rank possessing. ye who now will bless the poor, shall yourselves find blessing'.

With my maiden name of Gabbott being formed from two words meaning 'spear' and 'messenger'. My hope is that this book will bring a real message that will spear hearts for good and rekindle hope.

It is said that, 'Jesus did many other things besides what has been recorded. If every one of them was written down even the whole world would not have room for the books that would have to be written'. Even in writing my memoir, you simply cannot write about everyone you have ever known and all the things you have experienced.

There have been quite a few people along the way who have been wonderfully supportive of me and have been great friends over the years. I apologise in advance to anyone who may read this book who feels they should have had a mention in it. The memories unfolded as they did and with them the events mentioned. For those who have been mentioned, I have slightly altered names where appropriate to preserve anonymity as much as possible.

The problem with writing a memoir is that just when you feel the book is done, another memory pops into your mind. Usually, this is as you are desperately trying to fall asleep at night. It seems creativity flows best in that twilight moment between waking and sleeping. This often happens during the day too, when a thought comes to mind I have to open up notes on my phone and tap it in. If not then the memory fades and five minutes later it has often gone. And so these memories are now recorded to pass on to the next generation and for anyone else who may be interested in the stories and the facts.

It was whilst I was at Othona that this particular part of my journey began. I met a wonderful, elderly lady called Janet Wilkes from London. Her decorum and demeanour left a strong impression on me. We sat and shared a little of our lives and before she left, she handed me a book entitled, 'After the Blossom – my story by Janet Wilkes'. She had written her memoir and signed it, 'Dear Jo, showers of blossom, Love Janet'. I lay on my bed in the yurt and read it from cover to cover. It spoke of her life growing up in the changing scene of London over the years and of her strength and faith throughout it all. I emailed to thank her for her book and to tell of the way it had impacted me. She emailed back saying "Why don't you write yours?" and so I did.

I would love to hear if this book has impacted you in any way. Please email me at:- rekindlehopehouse@gmail.com

Printed in Poland
by Amazon Fulfillment
Poland Sp. z o.o., Wrocław